5/94

NEW THEORIES
ON THE
DINOSAURS

NEW THEORIES ON THE DINOSAURS

CHRISTOPHER LAMPTON

FRANKLIN WATTS
NEW YORK LONDON TORONTO SYDNEY
] 1989 [

Diagram by Vantage Art

Photographs courtesy of:
Field Museum of Natural History, Chicago: pp. 10,
67, 78 (all paintings by Charles R. Knight), 97;
Bettmann Archive: pp. 17, 20, 28, 50; The Granger
Collection: pp: 22, 36; American Museum of Natural
History: pp. 33, 42, 53 (bottom), 63, 71, 75, 86, 93,
100, 110, 122, 129, 131; U.S. Geological Survey:
p. 40 (G.K. Gilbert); Culver Pictures: p. 53 (top);
Denver Museum of Natural History: pp. 73, 114;
Natural History Museum of Los Angeles County: p. 77;
Dinosaur National Monument, Uintah County, Utah: p. 83.

Library of Congress Cataloging-in-Publication Data
Lampton, Christopher.
New theories on the dinosaurs / by Christopher Lampton.
p.   cm.
Bibliography: p.
Includes index.
Summary: Discusses new theories on the nature of
dinosaurs and how they came to be extinct, and details
some of the research that has provided the information
we have on these prehistoric creatures.
ISBN 0-531-10781-7
1. Dinosaurs—Juvenile literature.   [1. Dinosaurs.
2. Paleontology.]   I. Title.
QE862.D5L426   1989   89-31829   CIP   AC

CONTENTS

NEW THEORIES ON THE DINOSAURS

INTRODUCTION

Dinosaurs! Are there people so indifferent to the history of the earth that the name *dinosaurs* doesn't send shivers down their spines? Like the dragons of medieval legend, there is something mythical about these great reptiles. They could almost have stepped out of a dream—or a nightmare.

Yet, how much do we really know about the dinosaurs? They have been extinct for 65 million years, and this very fact colors our opinions of them. As impressive as they were, we tend to think of the dinosaurs as a kind of evolutionary failure, lumbering, cold-blooded beasts much too dim-witted to survive in a world destined to play host to the more highly advanced mammals—and, eventually, human beings.

But were dinosaurs really evolutionary failures? Certainly not! They dominated the earth for more than 150 million years, far longer than have

Was Tyrannosaurus rex *a
lumbering, cold-blooded beast?*

mammals, of which human beings are but a relatively recent example. The dinosaurs were im-
mensely successful, even though they did eventually become extinct.

In recent years, interest in the dinosaurs,
among the general public and scientists alike, has
reached a new peak. And a few renegade paleontologists—paleontologists are scientists who
study life in the distant past—have dared to suggest that the dinosaurs were much more advanced

in evolutionary terms than was previously suspected. Perhaps, these paleontologists say, the dinosaurs were not sluggish, cold-blooded reptiles at all, but a whole new class of living organisms quite different from modern reptiles. A new, sleeker, more sophisticated image of the dinosaurs is beginning to emerge, but it is a controversial image nonetheless.

In this book, we'll tell you about that new image of the dinosaurs; we'll also tell you why it is controversial. First, however, we'll show you how scientists came to their present understanding of dinosaurs; how the remains of the dinosaurs have become preserved beneath the earth in the form of fossils; and how dinosaurs fit into the 4.6-billion-year history of the planet on which we live.

ONE

DINOSAURS IN
DEEP TIME

Even at the beginning, dinosaurs were controversial. In fact, the very idea that the creatures that lived on the earth in the past were different from the creatures that live on earth today was controversial.

For one thing, there wasn't enough time. Until the nineteenth century, it was widely believed that the earth was less than six thousand years old. This figure had been calculated in the mid-seventeenth century by Archbishop James Ussher, who used the literal words of the Bible to determine that God had created the earth in the year 4004 B.C. In an age when such literal interpretations of the Bible were fashionable, Ussher's calculations had an almost scientific ring to them. But the very rocks of the earth itself—the rocks that Ussher believed were less than six thousand years old— contained the evidence that Ussher's calculations were very wrong. That evidence was in the form of *fossils*, from a Latin word meaning "things dug up."

Although today the word *fossil* refers to the remains of living organisms from the earth's past, it was originally applied to any nonliving object that was dug out of the ground, including rocks. But the most interesting of these "things dug up" were the ones that resembled the skeletons and shells of living creatures. Many of these were found at great depths beneath the earth's surface, unearthed in mines and quarries that cut like deep canyons into the rocks.

If the earth were less than six thousand years old, what were skeletons and shells doing at such great depths? No one knew. Perhaps the fossils were merely "figured stones," in the terminology of eighteenth-century fossil hunters; perhaps they had grown inside the earth itself, molded by mysterious forces into shapes that resembled those of living creatures.

By the mid-eighteenth century, however, this belief had become unfashionable, replaced by a conviction that the figured stones actually were the remains of living organisms that had died and been buried by the Biblical Flood, which had supposedly left alive only the animals and plants on Noah's Ark. This theory was deemed acceptable because, like Archbishop Ussher's calculation of the date of Creation, it agreed with the literal word of the Bible. It also explained why fossils were sometimes unexpectedly found near the tops of mountains, far above the ground. Presumably, they had been left there by the rising floodwaters, which had later receded, leaving the fossils behind.

In time, however, it was noticed that many of these fossils did not resemble, or only dimly resembled, creatures that were living on earth today. If the earth were only six thousand years old, how could the living organisms of the past be so different from the living organisms of today? Had entire species of plants and animals—not just individuals—been extinguished by the Flood, condemned to extinction because there was no room left on board the Ark?

No. This idea was not acceptable, because it implied that God had made some kind of mistake in the Creation, establishing species of animals that He intended to kill off at a later date. God, being all-powerful and all-knowing, did not make such mistakes. Living creatures did not become extinct. Therefore, living versions of these mysterious fossil organisms must still exist, surviving perhaps in some unexplored corner of the earth.

As late as the seventeenth and eighteenth centuries, it seemed possible that strange, undiscovered species of animals still lived in remote jungles and deserts, as yet unrecognized by European scientists. But as explorers pushed their way deeper into the jungles and deserts of Africa and the Americas, this became more and more unlikely.

In the eighteenth century, a Swedish botanist who called himself Carolus Linnaeus (a Latinized form of his real name, Carl von Linné) decided to create a catalog of all the living organisms on earth, and to classify each organism according to its resemblances to other living organisms. To give names to these organisms, Linnaeus invented the system of *binomial nomenclature* that is still used by scientists today. Each organism was given two names: a *generic name* indicating the *genus* to which the organism belonged, and a *specific name* indicating the *species* to which the organism belonged. Thus, the wolf, to cite a single example, is referred to in binomial nomenclature as *Canis lupus*, meaning that its genus is *Canis* (Latin for "dog") and its species is *lupus* (Latin for "wolf"). In the same fashion, the name for human beings in binomial nomenclature is *Homo sapiens*, from Latin words meaning "man the wise."

Today, we define a species as a group of organisms that can breed to produce fertile offspring. For instance, a male and a female *Canis lupus* can breed to produce a young *Canis lupus* offspring; thus, they are of the same species. A genus is a group of related species. Wolves belong to the same genus as domestic dogs. (In binomial nomenclature, the domestic dog is *Canis familiaris*.) However, because they are not members of the same species, dogs and wolves cannot breed to produce fertile offspring.

In addition, we now place genuses into a series of larger classifications, or groupings, some of which were developed by Linnaeus, some of which were introduced in later centuries. Genuses

*Carolus Linnaeus, the eighteenth-century
Swedish botanist, created a system that
is still used to classify living things.*

are grouped into *families*, families are grouped into *orders*, orders are grouped into *classes*, and classes are grouped into *phyla* (plural of *phylum*). Finally, the phyla are grouped into *kingdoms*. At one time, it was believed that all living organisms fit into two great kingdoms, the *plant* and *animal kingdoms*, though today we recognize that many extremely tiny organisms fall into kingdoms that are neither plant nor animal.

These categories, in turn, are sometimes broken into subcategories—suborders, subclasses, etc. Human beings, to give but one example of how this system works, belong to the species *sapiens* of the genus *Homo*, the family *Hominidae*, the order *Primates* (suborder *Anthropoidea*), the class *Mammalia* (subclass *Theria*), and the phylum *Chordata* (subphylum *Vertebrata*). By tradition, these names are all either taken from the Latin language or are Latinized versions of words from other languages.

Carolus Linnaeus lived at a time in which intrepid men and women were actively exploring the remote continents of the earth, especially North and South America and Africa. These explorers were captivated by the idea of a catalog in which all living creatures would be listed, and they delighted in returning to Europe with samples of plants and animals that they had found in their travels, so that Linnaeus could add them to his catalog.

Linnaeus believed that his catalog represented the very organisms, both plant and animal, that God had placed on earth six thousand years earlier during the Biblical Creation. By ordering these creatures in species, genuses, and other groupings, Linnaeus was demonstrating the actual organization of God's Creation, from the simplest of organisms to the one organism that stood at the peak of all Creation: *Homo sapiens.* Man the wise.

The notion that all living creatures belonged to a hierarchy leading upward from the crudest organisms and culminating in human beings is variously referred to by historians as the *Scala Naturae, Ladder of Life,* or *Great Chain of Being.* Although scientists no longer believe in the *Scala Naturae,* it introduced an important idea—that all living creatures are systematically related. And, indeed, they are. The reason for this relationship was not obvious in Linnaeus's time, however.

As more and more explorers returned to Europe with examples of organisms acquired in distant lands, and as Linnaeus's catalog grew accordingly, it became increasingly unlikely that hordes of unknown animals, such as those represented by fossilized remains, existed in some remote corner of our planet.

Linnaeus grouped the organisms in his catalog according to their physical resemblances. In the late eighteenth century, scientists discovered an even better way of cataloging living creatures: according to their internal organs, especially their bones. The science of cataloging living organisms according to their internal structure is called *comparative anatomy,* and the scientist who founded it

Georges Cuvier, here lecturing at the Paris Museum of Anthropology, was certain that entire species of animals had disappeared from the earth.

was the French biologist Georges Cuvier. It was Cuvier who discovered the true nature of fossils.

Cuvier was one of the most remarkable scientists of his time. He had the almost magical ability to identify an animal from a single bone of that animal. In fact, Cuvier could reconstruct an entire animal skeleton from a few bones, or even a single major bone, in that skeleton.

In 1796, Cuvier was presented with the fossil skeleton of a giant elephant discovered in the Americas. This skeleton, it was supposed, must have represented an existing species of elephant, because in the six thousand years since the Creation, no living organisms had become extinct—or so it was believed at the time. Yet, Cuvier was able to show that this was not the case. Using the techniques of comparative anatomy, Cuvier showed that this elephant belonged to neither of the two known species of elephant. Since it was by then considered unlikely that the unexplored regions of the earth harbored any undiscovered species as large as an elephant, the fossil skeleton must represent a species that no longer existed, a species that had become extinct. At a stroke, Cuvier had invented a new science: *paleontology*, the study of life in the distant past.

In the following years, many more fossil skeletons were brought to Cuvier, who systematically demonstrated that they belonged to extinct species. Some of these fossils belonged to giant extinct reptiles. One, the skeleton of a flying reptile, was dubbed *Pterodactylus* ("wing finger") by Cuvier. Another, a large reptile that had apparently lived in the sea, was given the name *Mososaurus* ("Meuse lizard," after the region in which it was found). Cuvier also identified an extinct species of giant sloth that he called *Megatherium*.

(You'll note that these are all Latinized generic names, in the tradition of Linnaeus. Unlike living species, which have common names such as "dog"

Cuvier worked from fossil skeletons, such as this one of an ancestor of the tapir, to reconstruct extinct animals.

or "cat" in addition to Latinized binomial names such as *Canis familiaris* and *Felis domesticus*, extinct species are known only by their scientific names. In this book, as in most popular books on extinct species, we will refer to various extinct species by their generic names—i.e., by the first half of their binomial names. The full name of one species of *Pterodactylus*, for instance, is *Pterodactylus kochi*, but this is very rarely used outside of technical literature.)

How had these creatures become extinct? Were they all victims of the Biblical Flood? Perhaps so, but there was evidence in the fossil record that there had been more than one flood—that is, more than one period during which fossil species had become extinct. In the late eighteenth century, a geologist named William Smith noticed that different *strata* of rock—that is, different layers of rock beneath the earth's surface—contained different fossils. Furthermore, these fossils were laid down in a definite order, with certain fossils always being buried more deeply than other fossils, as though they represented species that had existed at an earlier point in time. And this was true no matter where the geologist looked—in Europe, Asia, America, or anywhere else. In fact, it was possible to identify specific strata in the rocks by the nature of the fossils that they contained, so consistent was this fossil record.

Cuvier could only explain this by assuming that there had been a series of catastrophes in the earth's past, culminating with the Flood described in the Bible. Each of these catastrophes wreaked wholesale destruction on the living organisms of the planet, leaving behind only fossils to prove that certain species had once existed.

This idea, called *catastrophism,* was quickly seized on by those who wanted to reconcile the fossil record with the literal word of the Bible. Perhaps God had created life on earth several times, wiping out each Creation in turn with a disaster such as a flood, stopping only after He

]23[

had fashioned His greatest creation: human beings. (Obviously, there had been one more catastrophe—the Biblical Flood—after the most recent
Creation, but God had allowed human beings and
the other animals on board Noah's Ark to survive
that particular catastrophe.) The six thousand
years of Biblical history, then, represented only the
period of time since the latest Creation. Thus, the
earth could be older than six thousand years—
though probably not *too* much older.

But even as Cuvier was introducing the idea of
catastrophism—in fact, even *before* Cuvier introduced catastrophism—another idea was taking
hold. This idea not only explained the fossil record—why different fossils were contained in different strata—it also explained the very mountains
and canyons of the earth itself. This idea was
called *uniformitarianism.* The only catch was that
uniformitarianism required that the earth be extremely old, at least hundreds of millions of years
old. In an age that was just starting to believe that
the earth was older than six thousand years, this
was a radical idea indeed.

In 1795, a Scottish geologist named James
Hutton published a book entitled *Theory of the
Earth,* in which he took on the impressive task of
explaining the geology of the earth—the mountains, rivers, canyons, the very rocks themselves—
in terms of processes that could be observed in
modern times. Before Hutton, such phenomena as
mountains were explained in one of two ways:
They existed because God had placed them here
during the Creation, or they were the result of

great upheavals at some time in the past. This latter explanation was the one given by Cuvier's catastrophists. But Hutton pointed out that neither upheavals nor the hand of God was necessary to explain the geology of the earth; perfectly ordinary processes would suffice. Mountains could be formed by the same pressures that create volcanoes and earthquakes. They would then be worn away by the erosive processes of wind and rain and be ground down into particles that could be swept up in the powerful currents of rivers and carried to the ocean, where they would settle to the bottom and form new land. This new land, under the influence of pressures inside the earth, could later be thrust upward to form mountains. This theory neatly explained why fossils could be found on mountaintops—the mountaintops had once been at the bottoms of rivers.

These forces—erosion by wind and rain and mountain-building pressures inside the earth—worked very slowly. To explain the existing geology of the earth, it was necessary to assume that these forces had been at work for hundreds of millions of years, at the very least.

Few people in the late eighteenth century were willing to take seriously the idea that the earth was so tremendously old; thus, Hutton's book was largely ignored. But his ideas were rediscovered in the nineteenth century by another Scottish geologist, Charles Lyell, who published in 1830 an updated version of Hutton's theories in a book called *Principles of Geology*.

Hutton and Lyell had introduced a new concept into the study of life on earth, a concept that twentieth-century paleontologist Loren Eiseley would call "deep time." If Lyell and Hutton were right—and today we know that they were—then the earth has been around for a period of time so vast that the human mind cannot really comprehend it. Hutton, in fact, seemed to believe that the age of the earth might be infinite. In what has become a famous phrase, he wrote that when we study the earth "we find no vestige of a beginning, no prospect of an end." Today, however, we know that the earth is about 4.6 billion years old, such a far cry from Archbishop Ussher's six thousand years that the two figures can scarcely be compared.

The concept of deep time put the *Scala Naturae*—the Ladder of Life—in a new light. Linnaeus and Cuvier had shown that there was a resemblance between all living organisms. Once the antiquity of the earth was understood, a few scientists dared to suggest that there might be a closer relationship between these species than had hitherto been suspected. Perhaps, over vast periods of time and thousands of generations, it was possible for one organism to change—to *evolve*—into another organism. Perhaps all organisms had descended from a single organism, evolving over hundreds of millions of years to become the millions of organisms, both plant and animal, that we see about us today. If the earth were only six thousand years old, such a thing would scarcely seem possible, but with deep time many things became possible. Just as slow geologic change could create mountains, so slow change in living organisms could create new species. The process by which one organism changed into another was given the name *evolution*.

But what caused an organism to change? It was one thing to say that this change took place, another to show *why* it took place. The answer to this pivotal question came in 1859, with the publication of a book entitled *On the Origin of Species by Means of Natural Selection, or the Preservation of Favoured Races in the Struggle for Life*. More popularly known as *On the Origin of Species*, this book was written by an English naturalist named Charles Darwin.

In his youth, Darwin had traveled around the world on the ship *H.M.S. Beagle* and had explored the Galapagos Islands, off the west coast of South America. Darwin noticed that the animals on the islands resembled the animals that lived on the South American mainland; yet, they were also subtly different. Furthermore, the animals on each island were different from the animals on other islands. Darwin, who had read Lyell and was conversant with the idea of deep time, guessed that these animals had become isolated on the islands in the distant past and then had evolved into new forms.

Why had they evolved into new forms? On his return to England, Darwin read the works of the eighteenth-century English economist Thomas Malthus, who had observed that populations of

Once he had determined that organisms evolved over time, the next question asked by naturalist Charles Darwin was, Why?

human beings (and therefore animals as well, Darwin assumed) tended to multiply faster than their supply of food. The result was famine, war, or disease, which brought the population numbers back into balance. It was Darwin's inspired guess that this process also explained the changes that took place in living organisms over many generations. Only those organisms that were best adapted for gathering food within their environment would survive long enough to produce offspring; organisms not as well adapted would die without producing offspring. Over many generations, organisms evolved to become better and better adapted to their environment, simply because those who were well adapted produced more offspring. Darwin called this process *natural selection,* because it was nature itself that selected the best-adapted organisms and disposed of the rest.

But why are there so many different *kinds* of organisms? Why don't all organisms evolve into a single form best adapted for taking advantage of the environment? Because there are many different ways to take advantage of a given environment. Each of these ways is called an *ecological niche.* An animal that eats grass—a grazer—is not really in competition with an animal that eats leaves off trees—a browser. Thus, we say that the first animal occupies the grazing niche and that the second occupies the browsing niche.

Furthermore, there are many different environments, and each has its own set of ecological niches. The organisms that evolve to take advantage of a jungle environment, for instance, will be very different from those that evolve to take advantage of a desert environment or a grassland environment. A few extremely versatile animals can take advantage of a multitude of environments; human beings are probably the best example. Not only can we live in widely different environments, but we can alter environments that are not to our liking. (Alas, when we alter an environment to our liking, we often harm other organisms—plant and animal—that have evolved to live in that environment. But that's a story for another time.)

If natural selection selects the organisms best adapted for their environment, this would seem to imply that there are differences, or variations, between individual organisms within a species. And, in fact, we can see such differences just by looking around us. Not only do different species look different—an African violet bears little resemblance to a mosquito, for instance—but members of the same species also look different. We have little problem telling one human being from another, for instance, or the neighbor's cat from our own. But where did these differences come from?

Charles Darwin did not know the answer to this question, but today we do. When an organism produces offspring, it passes to its offspring a set of *genes*, special molecules that contain chemically coded information about that organism's physical form. There are genes, for instance, that determine the structure of bone and of eyeballs; and genes that determine the way in which the organism grows, the way in which it digests its food, and so forth. These genes are frequently rearranged by a natural shuffling of molecules called *genetic recombination*. Such changes are called *mutations*. Most of these alterations to the genes *harm* the offspring, making it less capable of surviving within its environment. These offspring will be discarded by natural selection, usually before they can produce offspring of their own. Occasionally, however, a genetic change will make the offspring *better* able to survive in its environment. Natural selection will select for these organisms.

Over long periods of time—millions of years—the collective effect of many different genetic changes can turn one species into another species. Thus, the numerous species on earth today probably evolved from a single organism that existed billions of years ago.

Darwin's theory was controversial when it was first published because it contradicted the literal word of the Bible, which says (or at least implies) that God created all of the species in their present forms. However, it is important to understand that Darwin was not denying the validity of religious belief. In fact, Darwin was a deeply religious man. He believed that natural selection was the tool that God had used to create the great variety of living species that we observe on the earth today. If there had been only six days for God to create all living organisms, as the Bible had stated, then natural selection would not have had time to do its work.

But in deep time, natural selection was a perfectly acceptable way to generate new species. To Darwin, and to many other scientists both then and now, the Biblical story of Creation was a metaphor for the way in which life was created, a parable rather than a literal history of the earth.

Today we take the concepts of deep time and evolution by natural selection for granted. Most educated people assume that the earth has been around for a long time (though most of us are unable to comprehend *how* long a time it has been) and that the organisms that lived on the earth in the past were different from those that live on earth today. But it's difficult to imagine how exciting these ideas concerning the earth's age and species changing with the passage of time must have been to people who lived in the nineteenth century. It was as though a door had been opened onto the past, and the room on the other side of that door had turned out to be vastly larger and more bizarre than anyone had imagined. In the beginning, however, there was not very much light in that room, and the history of the earth—particularly the history of living creatures on the earth—could be seen only dimly. And yet the clues to that history, the fossils buried within the earth, were available to anyone willing to search for them. For a few decades, it was possible for a geologist or paleontologist to walk a few miles from his or her home and find a single bone that would throw a dazzling spotlight into the mysterious room of the

*Gideon Algernon Mantell was an English
surgeon and successful fossil-hunter.*

past. Needless to say, fossil hunting became a popular hobby among bright young men and women.

In the 1820s, an English doctor named Gideon
Mantell, with the aid of his wife, Mary Ann Mantell, found one of the most dazzling spotlights of
all, a fossil that illuminated a vast stretch of earth's
history that we now call the Age of Dinosaurs.

ACCORDING TO a frequently repeated story, Dr. Mantell was called out in 1822 to visit a patient in the English countryside, and his wife, Mary Ann, came along for the ride. While the doctor attended his patient, Mrs. Mantell walked alone down a nearby country lane. Knowing that her husband had a strong interest in paleontology—in fact, she had drawn the illustrations for a book he had recently written on the subject—she kept an eye out for interesting pieces of rock that might contain fossil remains. Spying such a rock with a tooth embedded in it, she picked it up and gave it to Dr. Mantell when he returned.

Mantell found the rock very interesting. It was obviously quite old—today, in fact, we know that the rock must have been about 100 million years old—and the tooth that it contained looked like no tooth that Mantell had ever seen. It resembled a lizard's tooth, but it was larger than the tooth of any lizard with which Mantell was familiar. In fact, if the lizard from which this tooth had come was proportionately as large as the tooth, it might have been more than 100 feet (30 m) in length. (As it turned out, the extinct reptile that had once possessed this tooth was not a lizard but a quite different type of reptile; and it was not quite as large as Dr. Mantell had guessed, though it was still impressive: probably about 30 feet [0.9 m] long.)

At least one biographer of Dr. Mantell has suggested that much of the above story—in particular, the part about Mary Ann Mantell's discovering the fossil while her husband was on a medical errand—is legend rather than fact. Nonetheless, it is certain that at some time around the year 1820, Mantell did indeed come into possession of such a fossil tooth and that by 1822 he had recognized that it was a highly unusual fossil.

Regardless of how Mantell came into possession of this tooth, he then did what many amateur paleontologists of his time did when confronted with an unusual fossil. He sent it to the most eminent paleontologist of the age, Georges Cuvier, in hopes that Cuvier could use the techniques of comparative anatomy to identify it. Cuvier, however, disagreed with Mantell's assessment of the fossil. It was his opinion that Mantell had found the fossil tooth of a rhinoceros.

For once, Cuvier was wrong. Convinced that his fossil was in fact the tooth of a giant reptile, Mantell embarked on some paleontological research of his own, combing through the library in search of other fossils that resembled the one he had found. When a fellow researcher showed Mantell the teeth of a Central and South American iguana lizard, he immediately noticed a resemblance. On the basis of this evidence, Mantell dubbed his fossil giant reptile *Iguanodon*—"iguana tooth." Though he could not have known it at the time, Mantell had made the first reported find of a dinosaur. (As it would later turn out, fossil dinosaur remains had been discovered earlier, but

A nineteenth-century engraving shows a restoration of Mantell's Iguanodon.

Mantell was the first to recognize their significance.)

Even as Mantell was researching the background of his fossilized tooth, another English naturalist, William Buckland, had found portions of the skeleton of another giant fossil reptile. Dr. James Parkinson (better known for his description of "Parkinson's disease") named this creature *Megalosaurus*, or "giant lizard." A few years later, yet another large fossil reptile was discovered. This one was given the name *Hylaeosaurus*.

It was becoming obvious to nineteenth-century paleontologists that certain fossil strata—certain layers of rock—contained an unusually large number of reptile skeletons. Although reptiles represent a relatively small portion of modern living creatures (being restricted largely to tropical areas and outnumbered in the rest of the world by large mammals), these ancient fossils indicated that there was a time when almost all large animals on earth were reptiles. In 1841, the eminent English paleontologist Richard Owen decided that certain of these extinct reptiles—the ones that had lived on land as opposed to in the sea or in the air—deserved a name of their own, by virtue of their unusual size and posture. He declared that they had belonged to a previously unknown order of living creatures. Owen called this order the *Dinosauria*—the "terrible lizards."

—*TWO*—

THE FOSSIL
RECORD

In the years since Richard Owen gave the dinosaurs their name, paleontologists have cast much
light into that dark room of the past where the
dinosaurs lived. But today, even as in the time of
Gideon Mantell, the main link that we have to that
past is the fossil record, the vast collection of fossils
stored within the earth itself.

Where did these fossils come from? How were
they preserved for millions of years? How did we
come to find them now, such a long time after they
disappeared into the crust of the earth?

The answers to these questions may at first
seem obvious, but they really aren't. Nature rarely
works to preserve the remains of the dead. When
an animal or a plant dies, it is rapidly recycled back
into the environment, where the molecules of
which it is made can be used to build a new gener-
ation of living organisms. The carcass of a dead

animal, for instance, is quickly stripped of its flesh by predators, bacteria, and the erosive effects of weather. Even if it is buried beneath the ground, the skeleton will eventually be destroyed by the burrowing roots of plants and will become part of the soil.

Rarely are the remains of an organism preserved in recognizable form for as much as a year after it dies, much less for millions of years. How is it, then, that the remains of dinosaurs and other fossil organisms have come down to us over time?

Most fossils are preserved in *sedimentary rock*. What is sedimentary rock? It is rock that is formed by the accumulation and consolidation of particles of eroded rock such as those carried by rivers. Because sedimentary rock is so important to the fossilization process, let's take a closer look at how it comes into existence.

James Hutton and Charles Lyell showed how erosion wears away at the land, grinding rock into tiny particles that are eventually washed away by rivers. Many of these particles are small enough to become suspended in the water; other, larger particles, such as pebbles, may be rolled along on the river bottom by the force of the current. In time, the river will flow into a larger body of water, such as a bay. At this point, the flow of water slows and the particles settle to the bottom, where they remain. In time, other particles settle on top of these particles, and the weight of these overlying particles presses the earlier particles closer together. After the loose grains are compressed, minerals

*Layers of sedimentary rock may contain
remains of animal and plant life.*

can be deposited in the tiny spaces between the grains, eventually cementing them into solid rock.

Any larger objects caught up in this sedimentary rock will be trapped there forever—or until the rock is somehow exposed again to the outside world. This can happen when forces from deep inside the earth thrust the rock back above the ground, exposing the layers of sediment, or strata, laid down over millions of years. The rock is then eroded by the forces of wind and rain and its contents revealed to the world once more.

Sometimes the remains of a living organism

will be caught in the sedimentary rock. Over time, the soft parts of the organism will decay, but the bones will be preserved. In some instances, the actual bones will remain in the rock until they are eroded back out many years later. In other cases, the molecules of bone will be replaced over time with molecules of minerals carried in subsurface water, which will preserve the structure of the bones; this process, one of many modes of preservation, is called *replacement*. An organism that has been replaced by rock in this manner is said to be *fossilized*. In still other cases, the bones will decay, leaving a hollow space in the rocks that will be filled by minerals that seep through the surrounding sediment. If the rock is split at a later date, it will probably crack at the location of the vanished bones, revealing their impression in the rocks. Even a soft, boneless organism, such as a plant, can be preserved in this manner.

All such preserved forms are referred to as *fossils,* whether or not any part of the actual animal or plant is preserved. Even the impression of an organism on a rock tells us a great deal about the organism and the times in which it lived.

Not all living organisms are equally likely to be preserved in this form. Obviously, organisms that live in water are more likely to be preserved in the sediments than organisms that live on land, which is why some fossil beds contain an inordinate number of seashells and shark's teeth. However, the occasional land-dwelling animal will be drowned in a flood and swept away by its waters,

Spiral-shelled ammonites are common fossils.

will fall into water as it dies, or will die as it is walking through a water-filled swamp. Thus, a tiny portion of dry-land life will also find its way into the fossil record and millions of years later will come to the attention of a paleontologist trying to figure out what life was like in the distant past.

Although sedimentary rock is the most common place for fossils to appear, there are other ways in which fossils can form. Cave-dwelling animals can be trapped inside the earth after a cave-in. Animals walking through mud may leave behind footprints that will be accidentally preserved when the mud is overlaid with additional layers of sediment and allowed to harden with the footprints intact. Such footprints, in fact, are one of the most common types of fossil.

Fossils not only show us what prehistoric animals and plants looked like, but also when and where they lived. As William Smith first realized, certain fossils are restricted to certain strata of rock. This is because of the way in which the sedimentary rock is laid down over the ages. Newer rock settles on top of older rock, and thus the oldest fossils are preserved at the greatest depths. Each stratum of sedimentary rock represents an era of earth's bygone past, and the fossils preserved within it are the organisms that lived in that era. It is possible for paleontologists to fix a rough date—or, at least, a chronological sequence—on fossils simply by noting which level of strata they are found in.

In the nineteenth century, this was, in fact, the

only method by which paleontologists could determine the age of fossils. Unfortunately, while it was possible to gauge the relative age of fossils by their strata, it was impossible to tell exactly how old each stratum was, except by the roughest possible estimate. Thus, paleontologists gave *names* to the strata of rocks in lieu of dates. These names usually referred either to the geographic location at which the strata were first discovered or to some feature of the rocks and fossils found at that level. Thus, one of the oldest strata of rock is referred to as the *Cambrian* stratum because it was first discovered in Wales (Cambria being an ancient Roman name for Wales). Another stratum is referred to as the *Carboniferous,* because the rocks of that stratum contain unusual deposits of carbon.

In the twentieth century, it was discovered that ancient rocks could be dated by studying the changes that have taken place in certain unstable *radioactive* elements in those rocks. Because these changes take place at highly predictable rates, the amount of change that has taken place in a rock is a very precise indicator of the age of the rock. We can now assign dates as well as names to the strata and to the fossils that they contain.

It is still useful, however, to refer to the strata by their names as well as their actual ages, because the names that were long ago given to strata by paleontologists represent significant periods in the history of life on earth. The boundaries between named strata are often the scenes of significant shifts in the nature of the fossil record, the disappearance (or appearance) of whole orders of species. In this book, therefore, we will commonly refer to fossils by the names of the strata in which they were found.

The chart on page 46 lists the major names that paleontologists have assigned to strata from the last 600 million years, the period during which the vast majority of fossils were deposited in the sediments. The dates during which these strata were laid down are also included on the chart. Collectively, the names of the strata make up what is sometimes called the *geologic time scale,* a calendar based on the very rocks of the earth itself.

The geologic time scale is divided up in several different ways. The most recent 600-million-year period is divided into three long *eras:* the *Paleozoic* ("old life"), the *Mesozoic* ("middle life"), and the *Cenozoic* ("recent life"). Each of these eras is in turn divided up into *periods.*

The Paleozoic is divided up into the *Cambrian,* the *Ordovician,* the *Silurian,* the *Devonian,* the *Carboniferous,* and the *Permian.* The Mesozoic is divided up into the *Triassic,* the *Jurassic,* and the *Cretaceous.* The Cenozoic is divided up into the *Tertiary* and the *Quaternary.* The Cenozoic, because it is the most recent era and therefore has left a more detailed fossil record than other eras, has its Tertiary and Quaternary periods divided into epochs. The Tertiary divides into the *Paleocene* ("old recent"), the *Eocene* ("dawn of the recent"), the *Oligocene* ("slightly recent"), the *Miocene* ("less recent"), and the *Pliocene* ("more recent"). The

GEOLOGIC TIME SCALE

Time Scale	ERAS	Duration of Periods	PERIODS		DOMINANT ANIMAL LIFE
			Quaternary	Holocene / Pleistocene	Humankind
10 / 20 / 40 / 60	**CENOZOIC** 70 MILLION YEARS DURATION	70	Tertiary	Pliocene / Miocene / Oligocene / Eocene / Paleocene	Mammals
80 / 100	**MESOZOIC** 120 MILLION YEARS DURATION	50	Cretaceous		Dinosaurs
150		35	Jurassic		
		35	Triassic		
200	**PALEOZOIC** 350 MILLION YEARS DURATION	25	Permian		Primitive reptiles
250		50	Carboniferous		
300		65	Devonian		Amphibians
350		35	Silurian		Fishes
400		75	Ordovician		
450					Invertebrates
500		90	Cambrian		
Figures in millions of years	**PRECAMBRIAN**	Figures in millions of years	1500 million years duration		Beginnings of life

Only during the last 500,000,000 years have plants and animals produced hard parts capable of being fossilized. This is a simplified chart of that quarter of the earth's history.

Quaternary divides into the *Pleistocene* ("very recent") and the *Holocene* ("totally recent"). The Holocene covers roughly all of human civilization; we are still living in the Holocene today.

The entire 4-billion-year history of the earth prior to the Paleozoic is called the *Precambrian*. (The Cambrian, you will recall, was the first period of the Paleozoic era.) Very few fossils are ever found from the Precambrian, not because there were no living organisms during this time—it is believed, in fact, that life on earth developed near the beginning of the Precambrian, almost 4 billion years ago—but because life in this period lacked the hard shells and skeletons that are most easily preserved in sedimentary rock. Most organisms living during the Precambrian were single-celled organisms similar to modern algae or bacteria.

If the fossil record can show paleontologists *when* an organism lived, it can also show them *where* an organism lived, although this sort of *paleogeography* is not as simple as it sounds. Obviously, a fossil discovered in Europe once lived in the area that we call Europe today, and a fossil found in North America once lived in the area that we call North America today. But Europe and North America themselves weren't in the same place then as now. The continents of the earth have moved about considerably during the last 600 million years.

It was suspected as long ago as the turn of the century that the continents were moving. In fact, a few daring theorists had suggested such a thing even earlier but could offer no more than circumstantial evidence. The theory wasn't proven until the 1960s, when a mechanism was found to explain this *continental drift*. The earth's crust—the solid, rocky material that makes up the upper 20 miles (32 km) or so of the planet's surface—is divided up into a series of "plates" that fit together like a spherical jigsaw puzzle. These plates are floating on the semisolid "sea" of the earth's mantle. In the mantle, currents of hot material (magma) slowly rise like bubbles in boiling molasses, occasionally breaking through the crust at the bottom of the ocean, where the mantle is thinnest. When this hot material touches the water, it cools and hardens, becoming part of the ocean floor. This new ocean floor material forces the old ocean floor apart like a wedge, causing the crust to move. To make room for this ocean-floor spreading, there are other places, called *subduction zones*, where old ocean bottom is being swallowed once again by the earth's mantle.

The continents of the earth represent especially thick areas of crust. Unlike the ocean bottom, the continents are never swallowed in subduction zones nor is new continental material created by rising currents in the mantle; rather, the continents are carried about willy-nilly (if quite slowly, about 2 inches, or 5 cm, a year on average) by the motion of the plates. One hundred million years ago, all of the earth's continents were bunched together into a single supercontinent, which we now call *Pangaea* ("all earth"). If you look at a map or globe showing how the earth looks today, you can see how North and South America would fit neatly into the coastlines of Europe and Africa, almost like pieces of a jigsaw puzzle.

This, in fact, is how the earth looked at the beginning of the time of the dinosaurs. For years, paleontologists were baffled by the resemblance of fossils from ancient Africa to fossils from ancient South America, or the resemblance of fossils from ancient North America to fossils from ancient Europe. How could the same animals have lived on both continents when those continents were separated by impassable oceans? In desperation, they postulated the existence of long, narrow "land bridges" across which the animals must have migrated from one hemisphere to the other. Today we know that such land bridges would not have been necessary; and, in fact, they do not exist on the seafloor. The continents were once joined together.

NOW THAT we've considered the form that the fossil record takes, let's take a closer look at how paleontologists extracted the story of the dinosaurs from these fossils.

After Richard Owen announced that the ancient earth had been populated by giant, land-dwelling reptiles, European society went through a phase of what might be termed "dinosaur-mania." Dinosaurs instantly captured the public imagination. A sculptor named Benjamin Waterhouse Hawkins was commissioned to create life-size models of several prominent dinosaurs for display at London's Crystal Palace, a large building

*Richard Owen, English anatomist, devised
the name* Dinosauria—*terrible lizards—
to reflect the creatures' size and ferocity.*

left over from the Great Exhibition of the Works of Industry of All Nations, held in 1851. Alas, relatively little was known about the actual physical appearance of dinosaurs when Hawkins constructed his models in 1854, so his creations— models of *Iguanodon, Megalosaurus,* and *Hylaeosaurus*—lacked authenticity. Nonetheless, they were impressive, and some of the models have survived to this day. Later, Hawkins was commissioned by the city of New York to create similar models for display in Central Park, though the project ran afoul of a corrupt political administration and was never completed.

Dinosaur-mania began in England, but it quickly spread to the United States when it was discovered that the fossil beds of North America were, if anything, filled with more dinosaur remains than those of Europe. The first American dinosaur fossils had actually been discovered before the nineteenth century, though no one had realized what they were. (One set of dinosaur footprints uncovered in Massachusetts was mistaken for the footprints of birds.)

Joseph Leidy, who studied dinosaur bones uncovered in New Jersey, was the first great American dinosaur paleontologist. But the real dinosaur bonanza turned out to be in the American West. Colorado, in particular, turned out to be the home of several rich beds of dinosaur fossils. Throughout the late nineteenth century, these beds were the focus of a bitter rivalry between two eminent paleontologists from the East, Edward Drinker Cope and Othniel Charles Marsh.

Cope, brilliant but abrasive, and Marsh, methodical and dedicated, hated each other with a passion. According to some accounts, the rivalry began when Marsh pointed out to Cope, quite publicly, that the latter had placed the head of a reconstructed dinosaur on the wrong end of its skeleton. From Cope's point of view, it only aggravated the offense when Marsh turned out to be right. However, the rivalry between the two paleontologists was too passionate to have been caused by a single incident such as this. Perhaps it was simply a clash of two very different personalities.

In 1877, Marsh received several messages from a schoolteacher in Colorado about a large find of dinosaur bones near the town of Morrison. (The fossil beds at Morrison turned out to be part of an extensive network of fossils, now called the Morrison formation, dating from the Jurassic period of the Mesozoic era. These beds are still being mined for fossils by present-day paleontologists.) For some reason, Marsh ignored these messages and the schoolteacher turned to Cope for assistance. This galvanized Marsh into action. He acted immediately to keep Cope away from the fossil beds, a move which only inspired his rival to more desperate action. For the next two decades, the two

The Americans Edward Drinker Cope (top) and Othniel Charles Marsh (bottom) were eminent paleontologists who warred bitterly over dinosaur reconstructions.

paleontologists mined huge numbers of fossils from this and other sites in the American West. (Most of this was done by proxy, through agents on the spot, while Cope and Marsh analyzed the bones in comfort back East.) Each sent spies into the other's camp and attempted, sometimes successfully, to bribe the other's agents. The entire episode was an embarrassment to paleontology, but it produced a huge amount of data about the Age of Dinosaurs.

From the very beginning, bigger and bigger skeletons arrived from the West, each described by one of these eminent paleontologists as the largest that could possibly have existed, until another, even larger, skeleton arrived. Dinosaurs such as *Titanosaurus* (whose very name reflects its size), *Apatosaurus* (better known as *Brontosaurus*), *Camarasaurus*, *Diplodocus*, and *Brachiosaurus* must have towered over the prehistoric landscape. A typical *Brachiosaurus*, for instance, might have been 75 feet (22.5 m) long and 40 feet (12 m) tall.

Just as valuable as these dinosaur finds was the discovery in the fossil beds of the skeletons of tiny mammals, apparently the ancestors (or relatives of the ancestors) of modern mammals, including human beings. In the early nineteenth century, it had been thought that no mammals lived in the Age of Dinosaurs, partly because no mammal skeletons from this period turned up in the first beds of dinosaur fossils. But now it became obvious that this was not the case. Probably the mammal bones had simply been overlooked because of their small size relative to the dinosaur bones. Most of these mammals were about the same size as a rat or a shrew and probably bore some resemblance to these modern beasts.

After Cope and Marsh retired from the scene in the 1890s, other dinosaur hunters moved in on their territory. Even before Cope and Marsh retired, a budding paleontologist named Charles H. Sternberg wrote Cope a letter asking for a loan that would get him started prospecting for dinosaur bones in the West. Cope sent him $300, and Sternberg went on to become one of the great dinosaur paleontologists. Later he was joined by his three sons, George, Charles, and Levi, who also became eminent in the field.

In 1908, the Sternbergs made one of the most astonishing dinosaur finds of the century: a dinosaur skeleton accompanied by a perfect impression of the dinosaur's skin! Although paleontologists had previously guessed what the skin of a dinosaur might be like, this was the first time they were actually able to *see* that skin. The specimen, including the rock with its impressions of dinosaur skin, was later put on exhibit at the American Museum of Natural History in New York.

Early in the twentieth century, U.S. paleontologist Barnum Brown hunted fossils not only in the western United States but in the South American region of Patagonia and in western Canada. While exploring Canada for fossils, Brown set up camp on a barge and floated downstream, watching for fossil-bearing rocks on the shore. Irked that Brown was carrying Canadian fossils away to museums in the United States, the Canadian government enlisted the Sternbergs to come to their country for some fossil hunting of their own.

The greatest dinosaur find of the twentieth century, however, did not take place in the Americas but in Mongolia, an area that was then largely unexplored. And it took place only by a happy accident. A team of fossil hunters, under the direction of Roy Chapman Andrews (who went on to write many books on the subject of dinosaurs), had obtained permission from the Chinese government to look for early human fossils, which they never found. Instead, they stumbled on a great cache of dinosaur bones, including the remains of young dinosaurs (which are rarely ever found by fossil hunters) still inside fossilized eggs!

This expedition, in the 1920s, may have been the last of the great dinosaur-hunting forays, but the dinosaur hunters continue their activities even today. In succeeding years, Edwin Colbert inherited Roy Chapman Andrews' crown as combination dinosaur hunter/dinosaur popularizer, spending many years digging up fossils, then writing a number of excellent books about his findings. Today, dinosaur hunters such as Jim Jensen and Jack Horner still explore the American West looking for dinosaur remains.

These paleontologists have given us our picture of what life was like in the earth's past. In the next chapter, we'll take a look at the detailed picture that they have drawn, a picture that covers 4 billion years of life on earth—and of that particular episode in the history of earth that we call the Age of Dinosaurs.

═══THREE═══
LIFE STORY

The earth is approximately 4.6 billion years old. Even earlier, it was part of a spinning disk-shaped cloud of gas and dust in space, a cloud that grew smaller under the gravitational attraction of its own atoms and grew hotter as those atoms bumped incessantly into one another. Most of the matter in that spinning cloud became the sun, the glowing ball of hot gas that dominates the daytime sky. But some of that matter, in the outer part of the spinning disk of the cloud, clumped together to form the planets.

After it had formed, the earth was hot, and it took hundreds of millions of years to cool to the point where life could evolve. The early earth was very different from the earth that we know today. Its atmosphere consisted of foul gases belched out of its interior by volcanoes. A human being transported 4 billion years into the earth's past would find the air quite unbreathable, even poisonous.

Yet this atmosphere, combined with the strange chemicals in the primeval seas, provided perfect conditions for the chemical formation of molecules—chains of atoms—of the sort that are found in living organisms, the kinds of molecules that we call *organic molecules*. The hot rays of the sun, not blocked by the ozone layer that would later protect life on earth from the harsher forms of solar radiation, heated the seas (with help from volcanoes and lightning) and promoted the formation of more and more complex molecules. The earth, in short, was a gigantic chemical laboratory, and after 100 million years or so, a molecule appeared that could be called alive. This event must have occurred about half a billion years after the formation of the earth, approximately 4 billion years ago.

What distinguished this primitive living molecule from a nonliving molecule? Primarily one thing: The living molecule could make copies of itself. How can a molecule make copies of itself? Like the DNA molecules in the cells of your body (which this primitive molecule must have resembled), it probably built the copies out of smaller molecules floating loosely in the sea, using its own structure as a template, or mold, for the copies. This was not an intelligent or guided process; rather, it was an automatic process, like the functioning of a machine.

Once a molecule appeared that could make copies of itself—i.e., that could produce offspring—the process of natural selection, as described in Chapter One, began. As this *self-*

replicating molecule filled the primeval seas with copies of itself (which, in turn, produced copies of themselves), a primitive ecology emerged, with organisms (molecules) competing for food (smaller molecules from which to make copies of themselves). Errors in the copying process would occasionally produce new self-replicating molecules that were not identical to earlier molecules, and on rare occasions these new species of molecules were better adapted to this primitive environment than their ancestors. Natural selection would select for these new species of molecules. Thus, more- and more-complicated self-replicating molecules evolved. To see how far the evolution of a self-replicating molecule can go, just take a look around you. All living things on earth today, including human beings, are descendants of these molecules.

For roughly 3.5 billion years, life on earth remained in the sea. However, many important evolutionary events took place during this period. One of the most important of these events was the development of the *cell*. The first living molecules must have floated naked and unprotected in the sea, but at some point one of these molecules evolved a way of sheltering itself inside a membrane and taking food selectively into that membrane. Whether this first membrane was constructed by the molecule itself or was a natural formation into which the molecule moved, we do not know. But obviously, the membrane offered it a tremendous advantage over other living molecules, because all life today is made up of such membrane-covered cells, from the tiny one-celled organisms in a drop of water to large multicelled organisms such as human beings and whales.

All living organisms require energy in order to perform the activities, such as self-replication and food gathering, that keep them alive. The primitive living molecules received their energy from the sun, from lightning, and from volcanoes. But these energy sources are unreliable. What if the sun goes behind a cloud or the volcano stops erupting or the lightning stops crackling? At some point in the early history of the earth, a one-celled organism devised a method of storing the sun's energy in tiny molecules, in much the same way as we now store energy in batteries. By storing the energy while the sun was shining and cracking open the molecules to "release" the energy when it was needed, these organisms could stay active at all times. The process of storing the sun's energy in molecules is called *photosynthesis*—literally, "making with light." The organisms that evolved this process were the first plants. Eventually, other organisms evolved that ate these plants in order to obtain the energy-bearing molecules the plants formed by means of photosynthesis. These were the first *herbivorous* ("plant-eating") animals. Soon thereafter, other organisms evolved that ate the herbivorous animals to obtain the energy-bearing molecules, called *carbohydrates*, they had obtained from the plants. These were the first *carnivorous* ("meat-eating") animals. Thus was created the *food chain*, the process by which the sun's energy spreads throughout the world of living organisms. This energy is first trapped by plants through photosynthesis and stored in carbohydrates, then spreads to the herbivorous animals that eat the plants, and finally gets to the carnivorous animals that eat the herbivorous animals.

The development of photosynthesis had a surprising side effect. Plants literally changed the world. The chemical processes involved in photosynthesis produce oxygen molecules—chains of oxygen atoms—as a by-product of carbohydrate formation. The plants producing the carbohydrates simply released oxygen molecules into the earth's atmosphere. Initially, this constituted a form of pollution, because oxygen was deadly to most early living organisms. But, in time, new organisms evolved that could use this oxygen to help them "burn" the carbohydrate molecules from which they derived energy. Because these organisms could use this energy more efficiently than earlier organisms, they thrived—and helped prevent the oxygen "pollution" from reaching overwhelming levels in the atmosphere. In addition, special oxygen molecules called *ozone* formed in the upper atmosphere, screening out the harshest rays from the sun. This opened the way for certain simple plants to move from the sea to the shore, where previously the sunlight had been too intense for any living organism to survive.

At some point in this process, *multicellular* organisms evolved—organisms made up of more than one cell. The first multicellular organisms were loose colonies of cells acting in cooperation with one another, not unlike modern sponges. But eventually, organisms arose in which certain cells became specialized, becoming skin cells or nerve cells or other specific types of cells. These cells could no longer survive on their own, outside of the multicellular organisms of which they were a part.

In the last chapter, we saw that the first 4 billion years of earth's history, the long era that we call the Precambrian, produced very few fossils. Apparently, this is because there was very little about these soft-bodied organisms that lent itself to fossilization and the organisms were generally very small, making their discovery unlikely. Then, at the beginning of the Cambrian period of the Paleozoic era, there was a sudden proliferation of organisms that left fossils behind. The reason? Hard shells, and later skeletons, had evolved. The sudden proliferation of fossils at the beginning of the Cambrian is often called the *Cambrian explosion*, a name that gives some hint of what an abrupt change it represents in the fossil record.

Plants were the first organisms to escape from the sea and colonize the land. They were followed by the insects, the first animals to evolve a dry-

Fossils of the trilobites, which were abundant in the Cambrian period

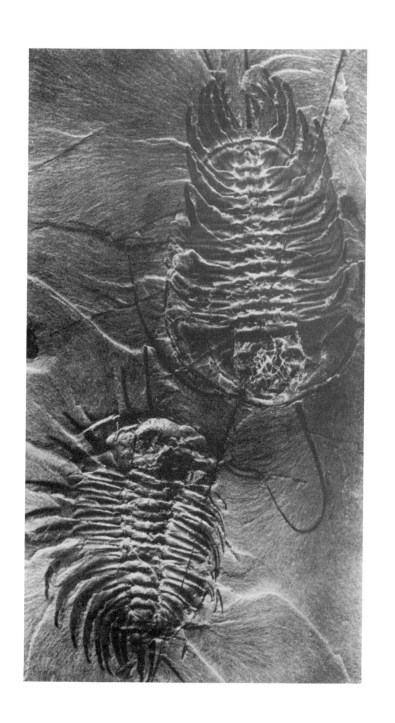

land life-style. The insects were also the first animals to evolve a means of flying.

In the sea, meanwhile, an important evolutionary development was taking place. Certain animals, called *vertebrates,* evolved backbones. The backbone provided a solid anchor for swimming muscles, and this allowed for the evolution of fish. Fish were the first major group of vertebrates. The Devonian period of the Paleozoic era is sometimes termed the *Age of Fish.*

Some places during the Devonian were subject to droughts and floods. A fish that lived in a narrow inlet might find itself trapped in a small pond when the channel of water that had connected it to the sea dried up. Fish need oxygen in order to survive. They usually obtain it from oxygen molecules that have been dissolved in water, but in a small pond, such as a prehistoric fish might have become trapped in, this dissolved oxygen might run out. A fish that could rise to the surface and gulp oxygen directly from the atmosphere would have survived when an ordinary fish could not. Such fish, similar to the modern lungfish, evolved during the Devonian.

Occasionally, a fish would find itself stranded on land when the pond in which it lived dried up entirely. Evolutionary processes would select fish that could survive on dry land long enough for rain to flood the lake bed and fill it with water again. Eventually, fish would have evolved that could use their fins to raise their bodies off the ground and "walk" to another pond.

Such fish, called *lobe-finned fish*, also evolved during the Devonian. Ultimately, some of their descendants evolved the ability to live out of the water entirely, returning only to lay their eggs, which would have shriveled if deposited on land. These were the first *amphibians*, similar to modern amphibians such as frogs and salamanders. The amphibians were the first large land animals. (A few "giant" insects also lived during this period— dragonflies with a wingspread of 30 inches, or 75 cm, for instance—but insects are not built to grow to large sizes and tend to survive better when their size is small.)

The move of large animals from the sea to dry land opened a wide variety of ecological niches. Food on the land was abundant; plants and insects were abundant. The amphibians dominated the dry land during the period we call the Carbon-iferous.

But the amphibians exhibited a major evolu-tionary disadvantage. They laid their eggs in water. This prevented them from moving very far from the watery environment in which their ances-tors had evolved and from occupying any ecologi-cal niches that were not available to an animal that lived in or near wetlands. It also put their eggs at the mercy of highly developed predators that lived in the sea.

The descendants of the amphibians evolved a new type of egg, the so-called *amniote egg*, which had a hard shell that held fluid inside and yet allowed the developing animal inside to breathe

the surrounding air. The amniote egg did not need to remain in water; it could be kept on dry land and could even be buried under the ground where predators were unlikely to discover it. These animals were able to move into a variety of ecological niches that had been unavailable to the amphibians themselves. The development of the amniote egg is such a major evolutionary change that paleontologists do not refer to these animals as amphibians. They call them *reptiles*.

The first reptiles probably resembled modern lizards. They were small and ate insects. However, their descendants evolved into two major lines. Some evolved into all of the reptiles that we know today—the turtles, the crocodiles, the snakes, and so forth—as well as several that no longer survive, including (as we shall see) the dinosaurs. Reptiles have been extremely successful, in evolutionary terms. Others evolved into mammallike reptiles.

During the Permian period of the Paleozoic era, the mammallike reptiles flourished. To modern eyes, the mammallike reptiles would have resembled reptiles, but there were distinct physical differences that distinguished them from true reptiles. They moved differently and their jaws were better constructed for chewing food.

The first mammallike reptiles were called the *pelycosaurs*. The most famous of the pelycosaurs was *Dimetrodon*, an animal sometimes mistakenly depicted as a dinosaur. *Dimetrodon* had a large, bony sail down its back that may have been used to control the animal's internal temperature. When it

Dimetrodon, *portrayed by Charles Robert Knight,
an American painter who created murals of dinosaur
life for a number of natural history museums*

turned its sail toward the sun, *Dimetrodon* would
have heated up; when it pumped large amounts of
blood into the sail, it would have radiated heat
back into the air. This whole question of heat control in prehistoric animals is an important one, and
we'll come back to it in the next chapter.

The second group of mammallike reptiles
were the *therapsids.* By the end of the Permian,
which was also the end of the Paleozoic era, the
therapsids were the dominant large land animals.

There were huge therapsids and small therapsids, carnivorous therapsids and herbivorous therapsids. In the world of 230 million years ago, therapsids occupied pretty much the same ecological niches that mammals occupy today.

And then, roughly 225 million years ago, something quite devastating happened. We don't know precisely what it was (though in Chapter Six we will discuss several possibilities), but it killed off most of the species of therapsids over a relatively short period of time, perhaps a few million years. Large numbers of species of reptiles and amphibians also died off, as well as most of the species that lived in the sea. This was the first of the great *mass extinctions* that paleontologists have noticed in the fossil record. There would be others in the eras to come, but to date this remains the worst mass extinction of all. So dramatic was this event that paleontologists use it as the marker for the end of the first great era of the fossil record, the Paleozoic. We now enter the second great era of the fossil record, the Mesozoic, the era that is referred to variously as the Age of Reptiles and the Age of Dinosaurs.

At the beginning of the Triassic, the first period of the Mesozoic, many ecological niches had been left open by the mass extinction. For a time, the therapsids seemed to recover from the beating that they had taken at the end of the Permian and again became the dominant large land animals. But by this time, a new type of reptile had evolved to compete with the therapsids for their ecological niches—the *thecodont*. The earliest thecodonts evolved in swamps and resembled crocodiles; in fact, they are the ancestors of modern crocodiles. They had powerful hind legs for propelling themselves through marshy water. When the swamps began to dry up early in the Triassic, they moved onto dry land. Their powerful hind legs helped them to spring suddenly on unsuspecting prey, such as therapsids. Soon the therapsids were on the wane, and the thecodonts became the dominant large land animals for most of the Triassic, occupying most of the ecological niches that had previously been occupied by the therapsids.

The most important evolutionary development of the thecodonts was their legs, which were kept directly under the body, instead of spraddled to the side as other reptiles' and therapsids' legs were. This allowed the thecodonts to move quickly and may have allowed a few thecodonts to develop a brand-new posture, previously unknown among animals. They could stand up, much as we can. These thecodonts, in turn, gave rise to yet another kind of reptile: the *archosaurs.* The archosaurs, or "ruling reptiles," included in their number the dinosaurs.

The dinosaurs were the thecodonts' undoing. Just as the thecodonts had previously moved into the ecological niches occupied by the therapsids, the dinosaurs now moved into the ecological niches occupied by the thecodonts. By the end of the Triassic, both the thecodonts *and* the therapsids were extinct, although the therapsids had spawned a brand-new evolutionary group, the mammals, which would one day evolve to dominate the earth.

However, that day was still a long way off. The Mesozoic era was the Age of Reptiles. During the Triassic, archosaur reptiles evolved and came to live in all the major environments of the earth. There were reptiles in the sea, such as *plesiosaurs* and *mosasaurs,* occupying the ecological niches that are today occupied by dolphins and whales. In the skies, flying reptiles called *pterosaurs* occupied the ecological niches later occupied by birds and bats. (Actually, birds and pterosaurs may have existed side by side in the skies of the later Mesozoic.) In the swamps, reptiles called *crocodilians* occupied the ecological niches occupied by modern crocodiles and alligators and were, in fact, the direct ancestors of these modern animals. And on the land, dinosaurs occupied almost all of the ecological niches that are today occupied by mammals.

What we call dinosaurs, after the fashion of Richard Owen (see Chapter One), are actually two groups of large land animals: the *saurischians* ("lizard-hipped reptiles") and the *ornithischians* ("bird-hipped reptiles"). Owen, not having access to the extensive fossil collections available to later paleontologists, had believed that these large reptiles were a single group. Later paleontologists felt that the differences in pelvic, or hip, structure between certain dinosaurs were sufficiently great to cause them to be classified into separate groups. A few

*Reptiles of the sea in the Mesozoic era
included plesiosaurs.*

modern paleontologists, however, believe that
Owen may have been right all along, that in spite
of their great variety, the dinosaurs do form one
large group of animals that can, in turn, be subdi-
vided according to hip structure.

Although we think of dinosaurs as being extremely large animals, the first dinosaurs were, in
fact, rather small. These were the *coelurosaurs*, and
they belonged to the saurischian family of dinosaurs. One of the coelurosaurs, *Compsognathus*,

may have been as short as 28 inches (70 cm)—and most of this length was tail. Discounting the tail, *Compsognathus* was about the size of a chicken.

The second period of the Mesozoic, the Jurassic, was the golden age of the large dinosaurs. During this 65-million-year period, the great saurischian dinosaurs evolved. The saurischians came in three varieties: the *theropods*, the *sauropods*, and the *prosauropods*.

Theropods were fierce carnivorous dinosaurs. In fact, they were the *only* carnivorous dinosaurs—all others were plant eaters—and included in their ranks some of the most terrifying predators ever to walk the earth. The most famous of the theropods was *Tyrannosaurus rex* (probably the only dinosaur popularly known by its entire binomial name, which means "king of the tyrant lizards"), though this fearsome predator didn't come along until practically the end of the Age of Dinosaurs, long after the Jurassic. Earlier theropods include *Allosaurus, Ceratosaurus,* and *Megalosaurus.* These particular theropods are also known as the *carnosaurs* and share a similar physical appearance. All stood on massive hind legs, had extremely small forelimbs, and had large heads with many sharp teeth.

The other major type of theropod was the coelurosaur, mentioned above. In addition to *Compsognathus*, the coelurosaurs included *Coelurus* and *Coelophysis.*

The sauropods were giant dinosaurs. At their largest, they were the most massive creatures ever

Tyrannosaurus rex, *the fiercest-looking dinosaur of all, displayed the characteristics of the theropods —massive hind legs and large, sharp teeth.*

to walk on dry land; only the modern blue whale, a mammal restricted by its huge size to an oceanic environment, is larger. The best known of the sauropods was *Apatosaurus*, better known as *Brontosaurus* ("thunder lizard"). Other sauropods include *Diplodocus*, *Brachiosaurus*, and some recently discovered dinosaurs tentatively (and quite unofficially) named "Supersaurus" and "Ultrasaurus." The sauropods had long necks, long tails, and pillarlike legs; unlike most other dinosaurs, a few sauropods had front legs longer than their hind legs. The bone structure of the sauropods was an engineering miracle, strong yet lightweight. The sauropods were anticipated in the Triassic period by the third group of saurischians, the prosauropods, which may have been the sauropod's ancestors.

At the end of the Jurassic, there was a sudden mass extinction that decimated the ranks of the saurischians. In the following (and final) period of the Mesozoic, the Cretaceous period, many new saurischians evolved, fiercer and larger than those in the Jurassic. But the Cretaceous was dominated by the second group of dinosaurs, the ornithischians. Our knowledge of the ornithischians' ancestry is scanty, but they probably evolved in the Triassic, remaining a minor branch of the archosaurs until the Cretaceous. There is some debate over how closely the saurischians and ornithischians were related. Obviously, they evolved from a common ancestor—all living things on earth evolved from a common ancestor—but no

Brontosaurus, *as drawn by Charles Robert Knight,*
had the long neck and tail of the sauropods.

one is sure if the common ancestor of the saurischians and ornithischians was a thecodont (the
ancestors of all archosaurs) or a very early dinosaur. Probably, it was a thecodont.

The variety of ornithischians was much
greater than that of the saurischians. There were
four major types of ornithischians: the *ornithopods,*
the *stegosaurs,* the *ankylosaurs,* and the *ceratopsians.*

The ornithopods, in turn, are usually divided

into four categories: the *hypsilophodonts,* the *iguanodonts,* the *pachycephalosaurs,* and the *hadrosaurs.* The hypsilophodonts were probably the earliest of the ornithopods. They were small and walked on their hind legs. The iguanodonts, of which Gideon Mantell's *Iguanodon* is a famous example, were tall browsers—that is, they were adapted for nibbling on the branches of trees and shrubs. The pachycephalosaurs, also known as the "dome-headed dinosaurs," had huge bulging skulls, which may have aided them in "head-butting" contests with other dinosaurs. And the hadrosaurs, also known as the "duck-billed dinosaurs," were the oddest of all the ornithopods, with flattened beaks resembling the bills of ducks.

The stegosaurs, also known as the "plated dinosaurs," are best exemplified by the dinosaur *Stegosaurus.* Like other stegosaurs, *Stegosaurus* walked on all fours. *Stegosaurus*'s most memorable feature is a double row of bony plates along its back. Paleontologists are still not certain precisely what these plates were used for.

The ankylosaurs, sometimes called the "armored dinosaurs," were covered by bony plates over much of their skin, rather like giant armadillos. *Ankylosaurus,* the best known of the ankylosaurs, had a clublike tail that may have been used as a weapon.

The psittacosaurs, also known as the "parrot-beaked dinosaurs," are notable for their deep skulls and large beaks, which—as their nickname implies—resembled those of parrots. *Psittaco-*

Stegosaurus, *reconstructed, displays a series of
bony plates along the ridge of the back.*

saurus, the best-known psittacosaur, may have
been the direct ancestor of the ceratopsians.

The ceratopsians, or "horned dinosaurs,"
were the last great branch of the ornithischians.
The most successful of the ceratopsians, *Triceratops,* may also have been the most successful of
all dinosaurs, if sheer numbers are a gauge of evolutionary success. By the end of the Cretaceous,
Triceratops represented nearly one-third of all the
dinosaurs remaining on earth. *Triceratops,* which

Triceratops, *shown by Charles Robert Knight, was perhaps the most numerous of all dinosaurs.*

had sharp horns protruding from above its eyes and a bony frill rising from behind its skull, may have been the prey of the great predator *Tyrannosaurus*.

AT THE END of the Cretaceous period, there was another mass extinction, the worst since the one at the end of the Permian. This was certainly the most famous of the great mass extinctions discovered in the fossil record, because it was the extinction that completely eliminated the dinosaurs. All species of ornithischians and saurischians vanished, though at least some paleontologists have suggested that the dinosaurs did indeed leave behind a descendant that still populates the earth, a possibility we will examine in more detail in Chapter Seven. The pterosaurs and plesiosaurs also vanished; the only surviving archosaurs were the crocodilians. Non-archosaurs were also affected; most of the life in the sea was devastated. As with earlier (and later) mass extinctions, there is no consensus on what caused this devastating episode in earth's history. There is no lack of theories, however; we will study some of the more notable (and controversial) theories in Chapter Six.

The loss of the archosaurs left a large number of ecological niches open for the survivors to evolve into—and evolve they did. From the human point of view, the most notable of the survivors were the mammals. The mammals had evolved during the Triassic, descending from the therapsids, the last group of mammallike reptiles. The mammals survived throughout the Mesozoic but never evolved into any form larger than a cat.

The early mammals were mostly nocturnal animals, coming out at night when the large reptiles were less likely to see them, eking out a living in a relatively minor ecological niche. But surviving in the shadow of the dinosaurs put the ingenuity of these tiny animals to the test, and in time they evolved a relatively high degree of intelligence, a trait that served them well as they became the dominant type of large land animal in the most recent era of paleontological history, the Cenozoic. The evolution of intelligence has reached what is thus far its apex only in the last few million years, in the development of the *hominids*, the line of mammals that led up to the appearance, only a few hundred thousand years ago, of *Homo sapiens,* man the wise, the species to which both the writer and the readers of this book belong.

THE ROUGH SKETCH of evolution given in this chapter represents the consensus, more or less, of those who study the prehistoric past as it is reflected in the fossil record. But the interpretation given to that fossil record is a controversial one. In addition, at the present time, there are few areas of paleontology in which the controversy is as heated as it is in the study of the dinosaurs.

In the next four chapters, we will attempt to fill in some of the holes in the story of the dinosaurs that we presented in this chapter, and we will show you why many of the questions concerning the dinosaurs and the ways in which they lived are still very much open questions indeed.

══════FOUR══════
HOT IDEAS

How nice it would be if we could climb into a time machine and study the earth as it was in the distant past! Like naturalists studying the lilies in the field and the birds in the trees, we could see firsthand what life was like in prehistoric times. We could scoop up samples of one-celled organisms from the primeval sea, shoot a dinosaur with an anesthetic dart and carry it back to the twentieth century in a cage, talk to a Neanderthal and find out once and for all if Neanderthals could, in fact, talk.

Alas, there is no such thing as a time machine, and, as far as anyone can predict, there never will be. If we want to learn about the earth's past, we must learn about it through the clues that the past has left for the present: that is, the fossil record.

But the fossil record consists primarily of bones and footprints, and there is only so much that one can learn from these traces of the distant past. Baron Georges Cuvier showed us that an entire animal can be reconstructed from a few pieces of bone, but Cuvier's science of comparative anatomy relied heavily on analogy. The bones of an unknown animal are reconstructed according to the rules that govern the bones of known animals. This works well for bones, which obey certain necessary principles of engineering, but it becomes chancier when the structure of the bones is used to reconstruct the soft tissues that once surrounded those bones or to determine how the animal lived back in the distant past.

Much of what we know about dinosaurs, for instance, has been determined by analogy to modern reptiles. Based on a study of their bones, dinosaurs have long been thought of as being reptiles, yet they are not quite like any reptiles alive today. Unlike those of modern reptiles, for instance, their legs were directly under their bodies, rather than spraddled to both sides. Also unlike modern reptiles, they were dominant in all parts of the earth and occupied all ecological niches available to large animals. Unlike modern reptiles—or any other modern land animal, for that matter—they grew to tremendous sizes; the largest dinosaurs, such as *Brachiosaurus* or *Apatosaurus,* would make an elephant seem puny.

And yet it is sometimes necessary, in the absence of additional evidence, to assume that in many ways the dinosaurs *were* like modern reptiles. Proof of these assumptions, inasmuch as any

The skeleton of a giant sauropod, reconstructed, provides clues for the study of the extinct animal.

intangible aspect of the ancient past can be "proved," is a matter of painstaking detective work, and such detective work can lead to heated arguments among paleontologists. One of the most heated arguments of all concerns, appropriately enough, the temperature of the dinosaurs' blood—or, more properly, the way in which that temperature was maintained.

What's the big deal about blood temperature? Why is this so important? Perhaps the single most significant difference between reptiles and mammals, the two dominant types of large land animals during the last 200 million years, is in the way that they maintain their internal body temperatures. Reptiles are *cold-blooded*, while mammals are *warm-blooded*.

Let's define some terms. When we say that an animal is cold-blooded or warm-blooded, we are not really describing its blood temperature but the way in which it *maintains* that temperature. When living organisms, during the Paleozoic, left the ocean for dry land, they left an environment that was in many ways much more appropriate for the survival of life. Water changes temperature very slowly, so that organisms in the water are not subject to sudden flashes of hot or cold. Once on dry land, however, living organisms were faced with violent fluctuations in the weather. Sudden spells of cold or heat were common on land, and living organisms were forced to adapt to them.

Heat is necessary for life because the chemical reactions that take place inside the living cell require heat in order to proceed. Without sufficient heat, an organism will slow down; in extreme cases, it will die. On the other hand, too much heat can also be dangerous, even deadly. If the chemical activities in the cell proceed too rapidly, chaos can result. The brain is the first organ affected by overheating; an animal whose bodily temperature soars too high will first become mentally addled, then will die.

All land animals must cope with these problems, but different animals cope in different ways.

Reptiles are said to be *ectothermic*—literally, "heated from outside"—because their bodily temperature is, to a large extent, at the mercy of their environment. In colloquial parlance, we say that they are cold-blooded, even though the temperature of a reptile's blood can be, under extreme conditions, warmer than that of a warm-blooded animal. In order to heat its body, however, a reptile must bask in the sun, absorbing the heat carried by the solar rays. Once it has heated itself, it may then indulge in a few minutes of strenuous physical activity, such as seeking prey. This activity uses up the heat, however, and eventually the reptile must return to basking in the sun. In cold weather, or on a day when the sun is blocked by clouds, the reptile will become sluggish and indolent, unable to generate enough activity to promote its own survival. This is why reptiles are more common in tropical climates than in temperate climates.

Warm-blooded animals, on the other hand, have tiny chemical "furnaces" within their cells that generate heat when needed. Thus, we say that they are *endothermic*—literally, "heated from within." Most warm-blooded animals also have methods of losing heat when they become overheated. Humans sweat, dogs pant, and so forth. This puts warm-blooded animals much less at the mercy of the weather and allows them to live in a wider variety of climates. The two major classes of warm-blooded animals are the mammals and the birds.

Dinosaurs, being reptiles, have traditionally

been regarded as cold-blooded. In light of this, there has always been a tendency to think of dinosaurs as relatively slow-moving, sluggish beasts, dim-witted and plodding.

In the last two decades, however, this assumption has come under attack from a small group of paleontologists, and this attack, which has often been loud and intensely emotional, has forced other paleontologists to reexamine their traditional views. Perhaps, the renegade paleontologists have suggested, the dinosaurs were not like modern reptiles at all. Perhaps they were warm-blooded, with metabolisms nearly as efficient as those of modern mammals. If so, they may have been fast-moving, energetic, and perhaps even a great deal more intelligent than paleontologists have given them credit for being.

Although the question of whether or not dinosaurs were cold-blooded is still very much an open one, it has become increasingly apparent that it is a complex one and deserves reexamination. Let's look at some of the facts—as well as the flights of fancy—that have gone into the debate.

IN A SENSE, the current debate began in the summer of 1964, when paleontologist John Ostrom of

Iguanodon *(model) and the other dinosaurs have been described as slow-moving, slow-thinking creatures.*

Yale University found the skeleton of a clawed hand in the rocks of south-central Montana. The hand was clearly from the skeleton of a dinosaur, and the teeth discovered near the hand were those of a carnivore, so the skeleton must have been that of a flesh-eating theropod. But the startling part of this find came the day after the discovery of the hand, when the bones of the dinosaur's foot were uncovered. The toes, not unexpectedly, were clawed, but the middle toe was different from the rest. It was larger and oddly shaped, rather like a sickle. Ostrom dubbed this dinosaur *Deinonychus*—the "terrible claw."

What was this sickle-shaped claw used for? Perhaps as a weapon, but its position on the foot made its utility rather problematical. For the claw to be of any use, *Deinonychus* must have attacked its prey while standing on one foot and slashing with the other, a position that would be difficult for most energetic, warm-blooded animals to carry off, much less a supposedly sluggish cold-blooded reptile.

Ostrom envisioned *Deinonychus* attacking its prey much as a martial-arts expert in a kung fu movie attacks a villain: leaping and kicking, slashing at its victim with sudden agile moves. But this didn't fit the standard image of the lumbering dinosaur. As Ostrom subsequently wrote, "It does not surprise us to see an eagle or hawk slash with its talons, or stand on one foot and lash out with the other. But to imagine a lizard or a crocodile—or any modern reptile—standing on its hind legs and attacking is ridiculous. Reptiles are just not capable of such intricate maneuvers, such delicate balance, poise and agility—such (metabolically) demanding activity. As we all know, reptiles are sluggish, sprawling animals that are boringly inactive most of the time."[1] Perhaps, Ostrom began to think, dinosaurs were not as typically reptilian as paleontologists had previously thought.

It was not Ostrom, however, who broached this idea to the world of paleontology. Rather, it was a student of Ostrom's, who had accompanied him on the expedition that had uncovered *Deinonychus*. The student's name was Robert Bakker. It is a name that has become synonymous with unconventional theories about dinosaurs.

In 1968, while working at Yale's Peabody Museum, the twenty-three-year-old Bakker published a paper entitled "The Superiority of Dinosaurs" in the museum's magazine *Discovery*. In it, he made the heretical suggestion that dinosaurs had very fast metabolisms, that they may even, in fact, have been warm-blooded. According to Bakker, dinosaurs "were fast, agile, energetic creatures that lived at a high physiological level reached elsewhere among land vertebrates only by the later, advanced mammals."[2]

The next year, Ostrom himself joined the fray. At a paleontological convention, Ostrom delivered a paper innocently titled "Terrestrial Vertebrates as Indicators of Mesozoic Climates." In the paper, he suggested that dinosaurs were quite capable of maintaining a constant body temperature.

He did not, however, suggest that they were *endothermic*—that is, warm-blooded. Rather, he suggested that they might have been *homoiothermic*, which simply means that their body temperatures were constant. As we shall see later in this chapter, this did not necessarily mean that they generated the heat from within, as warm-blooded animals do.

Nonetheless, the one-two punch of Bakker's article and Ostrom's paper shook up the world of paleontology. In subsequent years, a handful of paleontologists, including Robert Bakker, have searched for evidence of dinosaur warm-bloodedness, and some of their findings have been persuasive, if not conclusive. As paleontologist L.B. Halstead notes in his book *The Search for the Past*, "There is circumstantial evidence for hot-bloodedness in dinosaurs; when considered separately, each set of data is not overwhelming, but in conjunction with one another they can present a strong case."[3] Let's take a look at some of the "evidence" in favor of dinosaur warm-bloodedness, and the arguments that have been advanced for and against that evidence.

Predator-to-prey ratio. One of the most powerful, and controversial, arguments for dinosaur warm-bloodedness concerns the differences between environments that support warm-blooded carnivores and ones that support cold-blooded carnivores.

Carnivores—meat eaters—live at the top of the food chain. Unlike plants, they cannot derive their energy directly from the sun. Unlike herbivores—plant eaters—they cannot "steal" energy from green plants. Rather, they must depend on both plants *and* herbivores to process the sun's energy and convert it into a form that they *can* use—meat!

Creating a sizable supply of meat is no easy task. A typical herbivore takes years, and in many cases decades, to produce enough flesh to provide a meal for a few carnivores. A given carnivore will probably eat many herbivores in its lifetime. And thus, obviously, there is no way that an environment can support more carnivores than herbivores, or even as many carnivores as herbivores. In such a situation, most of the carnivores would starve. Thus, the predator-to-prey ratio—the ratio of the eaters to the eaten—must always favor the prey. There must always be more herbivores in an environment than carnivores, by weight if not by absolute numbers. (In theory, a few very large herbivores could support a larger number of very small carnivores, but this sort of situation is unlikely.)

The precise predator-to-prey ratio, however, depends on the metabolism of the carnivores. Carnivores that have fast metabolisms—that is, that use a lot of energy to support an active life-style—need more meat than carnivores that have slow metabolisms. Thus, cold-blooded, sluggish carnivores will usually represent a larger portion of a population than will warm-blooded, active carnivores, because they eat less. Therefore, a high predator-to-prey ratio—that is, a large percentage of carnivores relative to herbivores—indicates the presence of cold-blooded carnivores, and a low predator-to-prey ratio—that is, a small percentage of carnivores relative to herbivores—indicates the presence of warm-blooded carnivores.

On the face of it, it would seem a simple matter to examine the fossil remains of ancient environments and determine whether the predator-to-prey ratio in the Age of Dinosaurs was closer to that for warm-blooded animals or to that for cold-blooded animals. This should settle the argument over dinosaur warm-bloodedness once and for all. But, as usual in things paleontological, it's not quite that simple.

For one thing, the fossil record is spotty. As we saw in Chapter Two, not every living organism has an equal chance of being represented in the fossil record. Organisms that die in or near water, for instance, are more likely to become fossilized than those that die on dry land, and the fossil record from some eras is sufficiently spotty that guessing the ratio of various animals to one another is as much a matter of chance as it is of history. In addition, paleontologists themselves sometimes disrupt the fossil record. A paleontologist who removes only particularly interesting fossils from a site—those of especially impressive dinosaurs or of the particular species that the paleontologist is studying—may create a bias in the record. Anyone reading the reports of such a paleontologist might see the fossil record as biased

Fossil remains, such as this Tyrannosaurus
*skeleton, provide much information, but cannot
be relied on for population estimates.*

toward the species that were being collected and anyone examining the fossil beds at a later date will see a bias toward those fossils that got left behind. Neither will have a clear idea of what species actually made up the ancient population in that environment.

Studying the predator-to-prey ratio in modern environments is easier. For instance, in the game parks of Africa, where the carnivores are mostly warm-blooded, predators clearly make up less than 1 percent of the population. In 1970, using this ratio and painstaking research, Robert Bakker determined that the predator-to-prey ratio for certain dinosaur populations was 3 to 5 percent—that is, 3 to 5 percent of the dinosaurs (by weight) were carnivorous and the rest were herbivorous. This is higher than the ratio in African game parks, but according to Bakker it is not high enough to indicate that dinosaurs were cold-blooded; just the opposite. Bakker's study of the Permian period, when the reptiles and mammallike reptiles were clearly cold-blooded, shows a predator-to-prey ratio as high as 30 percent. Thus, the dinosaur ratio is closer to that of the warm-blooded carnivores in the African game parks than to the cold-blooded carnivores of the Permian.

Why should the ratio in the game parks be so much lower than *either* prehistoric ratio? According to Bakker, the game parks are an atypical environment. "The savannah covered by short grass is poor hunting ground because there isn't sufficient cover to allow the lions or hyenas to approach their prey,"

Bakker has written. "As a consequence, the predators are inefficient and do not catch enough prey to make an ecological difference, so the vegetarian herds grow bigger and bigger. And humans compound the situation. Herdsmen and ranchers kill off predators to protect their livestock. Poachers and pelt hunters kill for the skins. Hordes of tourists insist on harassing the predators during their hours of rest. In consequence, the Serengeti predators never build their populations to full potential. Is it any wonder why the predator-to-prey ratios are so far below the maximum possible with prey multiplying so abundantly and predators multiplying at such a minimum? Clearly, the predator-to-prey ratios of this modern game park are most unreliable guides for any understanding of the past."[4]

To prove his point, Bakker has examined predator-to-prey ratios in the more recent Eocene epoch, 50 million years ago. He claims that the ratio in the Eocene, a period dominated by warm-blooded mammals, was between 4 and 5 percent, almost identical to the ratio he observed among the dinosaurs.

Bakker believes that this alone should be the clinching evidence in favor of warm-blooded dinosaurs, but a majority of paleontologists disagree. Many argue that Bakker is simply wrong in his assessment of prehistoric predator-to-prey ratios; the fossil record is sufficiently spotty that Bakker is able to see in that record the ratio that he wants to see, based on his own belief in dinosaur warm-bloodedness. Other studies have shown results quite unlike those uncovered by Bakker, indicating much larger numbers of predators, as would be expected if the dinosaurs were cold-blooded. Thus, the argument from predator-to-prey ratios is inconclusive.

Dinosaurs had a warm-blooded "posture." As we have seen earlier, dinosaurs possessed a posture that is unlike that of any other reptiles. Their legs extended directly beneath their bodies, rather than sprawling to the side; many dinosaurs stood on their hind legs rather than on all fours. This resembles the posture of mammals and birds—both of them warm-blooded—more than it does the posture of cold-blooded reptiles. (In fact, the ornithischian dinosaurs are named for the resemblance of their hipbones to those of birds.) Although this by no means proves that dinosaurs were warm-blooded, it does suggest that they were built for greater speed than is the typical reptile and thus might have had faster metabolisms and therefore been endothermic. This web of arguments may seem a trifle weak, but it leads directly to the next argument.

Dinosaurs moved too fast to be cold-blooded. It would seem quite impossible to gauge the speed of animals that have been extinct for 65 million years, but in fact several attempts have been made to do just that. As we noted in Chapter Two, footprints are one of the most common types of fossils,

Brontosaurus *and other dinosaurs*
had warm-blooded posture.

and by examining the footprints of dinosaurs we can make some educated guesses about how quickly they moved. Here is how L.B. Halstead describes the process:

The length of the dinosaur's strides can be easily measured and from the footprint alone it is possible to calculate the height above ground of the hip and shoulder. Maximum speed cannot necessarily be determined, but it is possible to work out the exact speed at which the dinosaur was moving when it left the footprints. A large animal moving fairly slowly will take long strides, whereas a small animal moving fast takes very small strides. What matters is not the actual length of the stride, but its relationship to the size of the animal concerned. This is called the "relative stride" and is calculated by dividing the length of the stride by the height of the limb from the ground to its articulation with the limb-girdle. There is a relationship between the length of stride and body weight and speed.[5]

This is not as simple as it sounds, since the paleontologist must also know the species to which the dinosaur belonged, in order to calculate the dimensions of its frame. Nonetheless, by using special charts and more than a little guesswork, the paleontologist can calculate the speed of a dinosaur from the length of its stride—that is, the distance from one footprint to the next—and its weight.

What results have been obtained in this manner? Most dinosaur footprints indicate that the dinosaurs that left them were moving at a relatively slow speed, only about 2 to 3 miles (3.2 to 4.8 km) per hour. Does this mean that they were sluggish and cold-blooded? Not necessarily. According to Bakker, "most fossil trackways represent slow cruising speeds, not top speed, because all species spend most of their time moving along in an unhurried fashion. Bursts of maximum velocity erupt only rarely, when a predator charges or a plant-eater scampers for its life."

Still, one would expect that a few footprints

would show dinosaurs moving at high speeds, assuming that they were capable of high speeds. And, in fact, there is a collection of footprints in Australia that have been described as "a dinosaur stampede": footprints from 130 different dinosaurs apparently running for their lives from a predator. The fastest tracks seem to have been made by dinosaurs moving at less than 10 miles (16 km) per hour. A modern elephant, on the other hand, can move at speeds up to 25 miles (40 km) per hour, which makes these dinosaurs seem sluggish by comparison. A set of footprints in Texas, on the other hand, has been interpreted as showing a dinosaur moving at speeds comparable to an elephant's, and Bakker claims that *Tyrannosaurus*, when moving at a good clip, could run twice that fast. However, his estimates are extremely controversial and hardly represent conclusive evidence of dinosaur warm-bloodedness.

Dinosaurs lived in a wide variety of climates. Modern reptiles are restricted largely to tropical and semitropical areas. Dinosaurs, on the other hand, had spread over most of the globe. Does this mean that dinosaurs were better adapted for cold weather than modern reptiles?

Not necessarily. Climates were different during the Mesozoic, especially during the Cretaceous period. There was far less climatic variation between the equator and the poles. Warm weather would have been available farther to the north and south during the Age of Dinosaurs than

today. Further, the differences between seasons were less exaggerated; winters were milder and not much colder than summers.

And, lest we forget, the continents were in different positions during the Mesozoic. As we saw in Chapter Two, all of the earth's continents were once clustered together into the supercontinent Pangaea, and this would have been the case during most of the time the dinosaurs reigned. Thus, dinosaurs were free to wander across the entire planet, or at least that part of the planet that had land on it. If winter weather proved too harsh in the far northern (or far southern) latitudes, the dinosaurs could have migrated toward the equator, much as birds do today. In the summer, they could migrate back toward the poles. There were no major barriers to such a migration. In short, conditions during the Mesozoic were more conducive to a cold-blooded life-style than conditions are today.

Dinosaurs had "warm-blooded bones." Since bones are the most easily fossilized portion of an animal's body, it would be convenient if there were some obvious difference between the bones of warm-blooded animals and the bones of cold-blooded animals. If there were, then some clear sign of the animal's metabolism might show up in the fossilized remains.

Dinosaur tracks, here in a streambed, are used to calculate the animal's speed.

Some paleontologists argue that there *is* such a difference between warm-blooded bone and cold-blooded bone. It is in the form of tiny structures called *Haversian canals,* cylindrical passages that form in the bone as an animal grows. The appearance of these canals, in bone that has been sliced open, varies according to the speed with which the bone formed. In fast-growing bone, the Haversian canals are neatly ordered, like crystals; in slow-growing bones, the Haversian canals are dense and jumbled.

Studies of dinosaur bone have shown that the Haversian canals in dinosaur bone greatly resemble those in birds and mammals but do not much resemble those in living reptiles. Bakker and other proponents of the warm-blooded dinosaur theory suggest that this proves that dinosaurs were fast-growing endotherms.

But this thesis is torpedoed by the fact that the large mammallike reptiles of the Triassic had identical Haversian canals, and these animals are generally agreed to have been ectothermic. More likely, the Haversian structure simply indicates that the dinosaurs were fast-growing cold-blooded animals. Because of their great size, the dinosaurs must have grown very quickly—and thus the observed structure of the bone.

Of course, this fast growth may in itself have been a sign of warm-bloodedness. Once again, the evidence is inconclusive.

The descendants of dinosaurs are warm-blooded. There is a popular, if still controversial, theory among paleontologists that modern birds are the direct descendants of dinosaurs. We'll discuss this theory in considerably more detail in Chapter Seven; for now, suffice it to say that the evidence for this is persuasive but not clear-cut. It may or may not be true.

Birds, however, are unquestionably warm-blooded. Since birds did not descend from mammals—they clearly descended from reptiles of some sort—they must have evolved warm-bloodedness separately. Could they have inherited it from warm-blooded dinosaurs?

Even if birds did descend from dinosaurs, this does not prove that the dinosaurs were warm-blooded. Mammals descended from primitive reptiles, but this doesn't mean that those primitive reptiles were warm-blooded; almost certainly, they were not. Nonetheless, in conjunction with all of the evidence listed above, the warm-bloodedness of birds is suggestive.

SO FAR, we have discussed a number of arguments *against* dinosaur warm-bloodedness in our descriptions of the arguments *for* dinosaur warm-bloodedness. However, there are additional arguments against the possibility of warm-blooded dinosaurs. We will discuss two of them in the remainder of this chapter.

If Brontosaurus had been warm-blooded, it would have starved to death. Large sauropod dinosaurs such as *Apatosaurus* (*Brontosaurus*) combined massive bodies with surprisingly small mouths and small teeth. Warm-blooded animals have large energy requirements, and extremely large animals such as *Apatosaurus* would have had the largest energy requirements of all—if they were warm-blooded. This means that they would have had to consume huge amounts of vegetation. How did they find time to chew that much food with such small mouths and small teeth?

Bakker argues that some dinosaurs didn't chew their food—not with their mouths, anyway. They swallowed it whole and ground it up in their gizzards. Like certain birds, argues Bakker, the large sauropods made a habit of swallowing rocks, which tumbled around in their stomachs as they walked, mashing the unchewed food to a digestible pulp. In this way, even an animal with the staggering energy requirements of *Apatosaurus* could have processed enough food to support an active, warm-blooded life-style.

Is there any evidence that these dinosaurs kept rocks in their stomachs? Sauropod skeletons have occasionally been discovered with piles of smooth stones in the stomach regions. Paleontologists sometimes refer to these stones as *gastroliths*, or "stomach stones," but they may be an accident of the fossilization process. Fossils, as we saw in Chapter Two, are generally found where sediment has formed new rock at the mouth of a river, and in some cases these smooth stones may have accidentally become associated with ancient bones. Still, there is no way to prove that such stones were *not* present in dinosaur gizzards, and so Bakker's theory remains up in the air.

Dinosaurs didn't need to be warm-blooded. This is the theory of John Ostrom, who discovered *Deinonychus* and first raised the issue of active dinosaur life-styles. Most dinosaurs were so large that their bodies would have maintained a constant temperature even if they had not actively produced internal heat in the manner of warm-blooded animals such as mammals and birds. Rather than being endotherms, the dinosaurs would have been *inertial homoiotherms,* animals that maintain a constant temperature through passive means.

This conclusion is based on studies performed in the 1940s by U.S. paleontologist Edwin Colbert, who exposed a group of captive alligators to conditions of sunlight and shade, taking their temperatures all the while. Colbert discovered that large alligators heat up more slowly in the sun than do smaller alligators, but also cool off more slowly in the shade.

The reason for this lies in the so-called *surface-to-volume ratio.* Animals gain and lose heat through their surfaces—that is, through their skins. But they retain heat throughout the volume of their bodies. The lower the surface-to-volume ratio of an animal—that is, the less surface it has relative to the entire volume of its body—the more slowly it will change temperature due to external influences. Since large animals tend to have lower surface-to-volume ratios, they are also less subject to the temperature influence of their environments.

Ostrom suggests that the dinosaurs, being the largest animals ever to live on the land, did not need to be warm-blooded. Once a dinosaur heated up, it would have retained its heat almost effortlessly. This would have given the dinosaurs the best of both worlds. There was no need to eat huge amounts of food for endothermic heat production, but the heat retained by their large bodies would have allowed them to be active and fast-moving, almost like warm-blooded animals.

This theory has a satisfying ring to it, but it overlooks one thing: Not all dinosaurs were large. Many dinosaurs were no larger than horses or cows; some, as we have seen, were as small as chickens. *Deinonychus,* which Ostrom used as his model for the new, more active picture of the dinosaur, was minuscule compared to the giant sauropods. How did these smaller dinosaurs maintain their body heat?

As of yet, Ostrom has provided no answer.

IN SOME WAYS, it is tempting to think of the mighty dinosaurs as being relatively advanced warm-blooded animals. But it is important to bear in mind that theories of dinosaur warm-bloodedness are very much unproven. They are controversial today, and will probably remain controversial for some time. If more solid evidence for dinosaur warm-bloodedness is not uncovered, the idea will probably fade away with time, thrown onto the junk pile of interesting ideas that never quite worked out. On the other hand, future paleontologists may discover additional evidence that will make the possibility of dinosaur warm-bloodedness seem more likely than it does at present. It is really too early to predict.

Robert Bakker, who is the paleontologist most closely identified with these theories, is a controversial figure. His former teacher, John Ostrom, who has backed away from Bakker's more radical theories of dinosaur metabolism, has written of Bakker: "Such outrageous claims have so diminished Bakker's scientific credibility that many paleontologists and other scientists have stopped taking him seriously. . . ."[6]

Yet Bakker has his supporters. They are sometimes appalled at the feistiness with which he attacks what he calls the "old guard" of paleontology, or his tendency to advocate theories far from the mainstream of paleontological thought. But only time, and the slow process of accumulating fossil evidence about the distant past, will show whether Bakker's theories are right or wrong.

FIVE

LIFE-STYLES OF THE LARGE AND EXTINCT

Not all of the new theories of dinosaurs concern the ways in which dinosaurs maintained their internal temperatures. In the last twenty years or so, paleontologists have been forced to rethink some of their ideas about how dinosaurs lived—how they raised their young, where they lived, even how they walked. Some of these ideas bear on the question of dinosaur warm-bloodedness, others do not. In this chapter, we'll look at several of these new theories of the dinosaurs' life-style.

Did dinosaurs give birth to live offspring? As we saw in Chapter Three, one of the great evolutionary innovations of the reptiles was the amniote egg, the hard-shelled egg that allowed reptiles to protect their young from predators and to live at a distance from water. Birds, which descended from reptiles, also lay hard-shelled eggs. Even today, reptiles reproduce by laying eggs. Naturally, it was assumed initially that dinosaurs reproduced in the same fashion. And, in fact, fossilized dinosaur eggs have been discovered on several occasions.

All but the most primitive mammals, on the other hand, give birth to live young. This has an important, even profound, effect on mammalian life-styles. Infant mammals require parental protection for months, even years, after birth. (Humans, who require more than a decade of parental protection, are an extreme case.) This, in turn, has encouraged mammals to develop a close-knit form of society. Parents cannot simply abandon their children immediately after birth.

There is evidence, in fact, that some dinosaurs may have given birth to live young. *Apatosaurus*, for instance, had a sufficiently large opening in its pelvis for a baby sauropod to have emerged. And no fossilized *Apatosaurus* eggs have ever been discovered. Bakker suggests that this would have allowed baby sauropods to be quite large—larger than if they had been born from eggs because very large eggs simply aren't feasible.

This may have some bearing on the following question.

Did dinosaurs nurture their young? Modern reptiles are not known for their close-knit families. Most lay eggs and then abandon them, not waiting around to see what their children are like. A few guard the eggs until they hatch, then leave. Almost none raise the children after they are born

(nor are they required to; the young are fully viable as hatchlings). Mammals, on the other hand, are quite solicitous of their young, as are birds. Dinosaurs have traditionally been thought to follow the reptilian pattern.

In recent years, evidence has been found that even the egg-laying dinosaurs may have spent more time with their children than was previously thought to be the case. In 1978, dinosaur hunters Jack Horner and Bob Makela made an astonishing find in a fossil-bearing rock unit in Montana called the Two Medicine Formation: a dinosaur "nest" containing not only the eggs of a new species of hadrosaur, but the fossilized remains of the baby dinosaurs themselves—some of them still in the eggs! A year later, Horner made a similar find at a nearby site, once again discovering fossilized eggs with the skeletons of young dinosaurs—hypsilophodonts, in this case—both in and around the eggs.

In itself, this was one of the most remarkable dinosaur finds in paleontological history, but it also held exciting implications on the subject of dinosaur family life. Because not all of the baby dinosaurs were still in the eggs, it was apparent that the newborn dinosaurs remained in the vicinity of the nests, where they were presumably

A nest of fossilized dinosaur eggs is evidence that some dinosaurs reproduced by laying eggs.

protected by the adult dinosaurs. Horner hypothesizes that the young dinosaurs died when the parent dinosaurs were unable to return to the nest with their food. The baby dinosaurs remained in the nest and starved to death. Because these species obviously cared for their young after they were born, Horner named the new species of hadrosaurs *Maiasaura*, the "good mother lizard."

Dinosaur eggs are a rare find. Surprisingly, young dinosaurs are also fairly rare in the fossil record. In part, this may be explained by the fast growth rates and relatively long life-spans of the dinosaurs, but Horner has an additional explanation. He believes that dinosaurs generally raised their young in environments far away from those where the majority of dinosaurs lived, in order to minimize the chance of their babies falling prey to carnivores. Paleontologists like to look for fossils in areas where dinosaurs were common; hence, they miss the fossil remains of young dinosaurs, which would be in the areas where dinosaur fossils are relatively uncommon.

Could sauropods support their own weight on dry land? The sauropods—*Brachiosaurus, Apatosaurus* (*Brontosaurus*), *Diplodocus,* and their relatives— were the largest land animals of all time. This fact has led many paleontologists, from Cope and Marsh to the present day, to suggest that they occupied an aquatic or semiaquatic niche, submersing themselves in water to gain support for their tremendous bulk and rising to the surface only to breathe air.

Certain features of the sauropod anatomy would seem to support this theory. The sauropod nostrils tend to be on the very top of the head, so that the animals would have been able to breathe with almost their entire bodies submerged. Further, their long necks would have allowed them to walk through fairly deep water without losing touch with the surface. There are even fossilized *Apatosaurus* footprints indicating that the creature was walking on its front legs alone, using the hind legs only to change direction, as though it were swimming.

Given the sauropods' tremendous size, it is not unreasonable to assume that they might have needed a little help getting around. Furthermore, watery surroundings would have protected the sauropods from attacking carnosaurs. But in recent years, this theory has become untenable. Research has shown that, in fact, the water pressure would have crushed the sauropods' lungs. They would have been unable to breathe.

Under the old theory, the sauropods were assumed to live by eating seaweed off the bottom of lakes. The new theory opens up more exciting ecological possibilities. More likely, the sauropods were the Mesozoic equivalents of giraffes. They lived by grazing off tall trees, their long necks allowing them to reach vegetation unavailable to punier dinosaurs.

Did dinosaurs "speak"? No one has seriously suggested that dinosaurs had any form of language, but there is some controversy over the noises that

Diplodocus *and other sauropods may have
used their long necks to graze on trees.*

dinosaurs may or may not have made. We saw in
Chapter Three that the hadrosaurs were endowed
with rather bizarre "helmets," or crests, atop their
heads. The debate over what role these crests
played has raged on for years without reaching a
satisfactory conclusion. One of the leading theories
is that the crests were resonating chambers with
which the dinosaurs made honking or tooting
noises, a kind of reptilian French horn.

Why would dinosaurs have made honking
noises? One possibility is that the sounds would
have allowed a hadrosaur to alert other members
of the herd to the presence of an attacking car-
nosaur. But a more interesting possibility is that
the sounds—and the musical crests with which
they made those sounds—rendered the male
hadrosaurs more attractive to female hadrosaurs.
Darwin himself recognized that certain animals
develop features, through natural selection, that
improve their chances of mating with a member of
the opposite sex; he called this process *sexual selec-*

tion. Male hadrosaurs may have engaged in honking contests to woo a prospective mate, a sort of dinosaur serenade.

In addition, a large crest may have helped the male hadrosaurs to intimidate one another when vying for the affection of a female. Quite possibly, this also explains the dome-shaped heads of the pachycephalosaurs. They may have engaged in ritual head-butting contests, contending for the privilege of mating with a female dinosaur. Many modern animals, such as elk, engage in similar contests, grappling among themselves with fearsome arrangements of antlers.

Robert Bakker uses this explanation as yet another clue to dinosaur warm-bloodedness. If dinosaurs did engage in such courtship rituals, it would indicate that they had energy to burn and therefore must have been endothermic.

━━━━━*SIX*━━━━━
EXEUNT REPTILES,
STAGE LEFT

If the dinosaurs were such advanced organisms, where are they today?

Indeed, whether or not the dinosaurs were warm-blooded, their disappearance is one of the great mysteries of paleontology. The great Cretaceous extinction is a puzzle for which a satisfactory solution has yet to be found.

At the very top of the fossil strata representing the Mesozoic era, there is a sudden violent alteration in the fossil record, the most extensive since the one at the top of the Paleozoic strata. At least half of the species living on earth suddenly vanish from the record. A huge number of ecological niches fall open and are filled again in the lowest Cenozoic strata by mammals rather than reptiles.

All of the saurischians and ornithischians died out. In fact, all of the archosaurs except for the crocodilians became extinct. Ocean life, from microscopic life-forms to the largest seagoing reptiles, was devastated. On the other hand, the mammals survived, as did most land plants. What sort of event would have eliminated life-forms so selectively, yet devastatingly?

No one knows, but there are theories. There are many, *many* theories, most of them contradictory. In 1964, scientist-author Glenn L. Jepson summarized the extant theories of the so-called terminal Cretaceous event in one memorable, oft-quoted paragraph:

Authors with varying competence have suggested that dinosaurs disappeared because the climate deteriorated (became suddenly or slowly too hot or cold or dry or wet), or that the diet did (with too much food or not enough of such substances as fern oil; from poisons in water or plants or ingested minerals; by bankruptcy of calcium or other necessary elements). Other writers have put the blame on disease, parasites, wars, anatomical or metabolic disorders (slipped vertebral discs, malfunction or imbalance of hormone and endocrine systems, dwindling brain and consequent stupidity, heat sterilization, effects of being warm-blooded in the Mesozoic world), racial old age, evolutionary drift into senescent overspecialization, changes in the pressure or composition of the atmosphere, poison gases, volcanic dust, excessive oxygen from plants, meteorites, comets, gene pool drainage by little mammalian egg-eaters, overkill capacity by predators, fluctuation of gravitational constants, development of psychotic suicidal

factors, entropy, cosmic radiation, shift of Earth's rota-
tional poles, floods, continental drift, extraction of the
moon from the Pacific Basin, drainage of swamp and
lake environments, sunspots, God's will, mountain
building, raids by little green hunters in flying saucers,
lack of even standing room in Noah's Ark, and paleo-
weltschmerz.7

Since Jepson wrote that paragraph, even more theories have emerged—along with some startling
evidence in favor of those theories. In this chapter,
we'll discuss two of the most popular current theories of why the dinosaurs became extinct: changes
in the earth's geography, and a bombardment of
asteroids or comets from outer space. Because the
latter theory is enjoying the greatest popularity at
the moment, we'll examine it first.

THE EVIDENCE for the so-called impact extinction
theory—the idea that dinosaurs and other Mesozoic life-forms were killed by an asteroid or a
comet striking the earth—was uncovered in the
1970s by geologist Walter Alvarez. In the sedimentary rock of Gubbio, Italy, Alvarez found a layer of
clay that marked the end of the Cretaceous period.
When this clay was analyzed by a team of scientists at Lawrence Berkeley Laboratory in Califor-
nia—a team that included both Alvarez and his
father, Nobel prize–winning physicist Luis W. Alvarez, along with chemists Helen V. Michel and
Frank Asaro—it was discovered to contain an unusually large amount of an element called iridium,
which is rarely found in sediment.

Where did this "iridium anomaly" come from? Although iridium is rare on the surface of the earth, it is relatively common in meteors. Perhaps, the Alvarez team hypothesized, the iridium had come from space.

The team considered several possible scenarios for the arrival of the iridium on earth, and the only one that made sense was that a large, iridium-rich meteor—probably an asteroid that had wandered far from the Asteroid Belt between Mars and Jupiter—had collided with the earth. According to their computer simulations, such a collision would have raised huge clouds of dust (and steam, if it had struck the ocean), which would have remained in the upper atmosphere for several months, even years. Such clouds would have blocked the sun, shutting down photosynthesis in plants and temporarily disrupting the food chain. Wholesale loss of life would have resulted.

This theory is not totally embraced even today by paleontologists, who have always viewed the Cretaceous extinction as a gradual event, taking place over millions of years. Indeed, the fossil record was traditionally accepted as showing a slow deterioration of Mesozoic life-forms—in particular, the dinosaurs—throughout the latter part of the Cretaceous. But the iridium anomaly was a solid piece of evidence in favor of the Alvarez theory, and other geologists soon turned up evidence of additional iridium anomalies in fossil beds around the world. In addition, tiny bits of glassy rock called *microtektites*, apparently formed by intense heating of rock, were discovered. Could these have been created in the meteor collision?

Other theories were advanced to explain the iridium anomaly and the microtektites, but only one gained any acceptance. Geologists Charles B. Officer and Charles L. Drake of Dartmouth hypothesized that the late Cretaceous was a time of unusual volcanic activity that placed dark clouds of volcanic ash in the upper atmosphere and resulted in much the same breakdown of the food chain as the Alvarez team was suggesting, but over a longer period of time.

This would help to explain the drawn-out extinction shown by the fossil record. Supporters of the Alvarez impact theory suggest that the asteroid merely provided the *coup de grace* for the dinosaurs, who were already on the decline for other reasons.

The Cretaceous extinction, however, is not the only extinction in the fossil record. Is it possible that other extinctions, such as the minor one at the end of the Jurassic and the major one at the end of the Permian, could have been caused by meteors?

Scientists were not slow to advance such theories, and some evidence for iridium anomalies in other strata was reported. The results of such research, however, were inconclusive. Then, in 1983, two paleontologists from the University of Chicago, David M. Raup and J. John Sepkoski, Jr., announced that they had found evidence in the fossil record that there had been many more mass extinctions than had previously been realized—and that the extinctions seemed to be appearing on a regular schedule!

Sepkoski was studying marine extinctions—the extinctions of some families of organisms that lived in the sea. With his colleague Raup, he graphed these extinctions on a computer and discovered that the number of extinctions went up noticeably every twenty-six million years, beginning with the extinction at the end of the Permian. (The data with which Raup and Sepkoski were working did not include figures for the earlier Paleozoic era.)

What was causing these *periodic mass extinctions?* There are no known earthly cycles that take twenty-six million years to recur, so it was inevitable that Raup and Sepkoski's colleagues would turn to extraterrestrial explanations. Perhaps, it was suggested, something in space was causing these extinctions.

This fit in neatly with the Alvarez impact hypothesis. What if the earth were being periodically bombarded by large meteors?

But this theory required a large source of such meteors that could be induced, every twenty-six million years, to pelt the earth. And, in fact, such a source may exist—if it is assumed that the meteors are not asteroids but comets.

Comets are large chunks of ice and dust that orbit around the sun in extremely stretched-out ellipses. Some comets return to the vicinity of the sun on a regular schedule, passing close to the sun at one end of their orbits and moving far away from it at the other end. The famous Halley's comet, for instance, returns to the sun every seventy-six years, flashing briefly through the skies of earth,

then disappearing into the outer solar system, where it passes near the planet Jupiter.

Most scientists believe that the comets come from a large cloud of ice chunks surrounding the sun at a distance much greater than that of the orbit of Pluto. This cloud, called the *Oort cloud*, after the astronomer who first suggested its existence, is periodically agitated by the gravity of passing stars, and this agitation sends pieces of the cloud falling toward the inner solar system, where they become comets.

Could something be agitating the Oort cloud every twenty-six million years? Certainly, this was a possibility, but the source of the alleged agitation was not known.

Several theories were advanced to explain the agitation. The most notable, and by far the most intriguing, is the so-called death star theory, which suggests that the sun is part of a double-star system. Since most stars visible to astronomers are part of such systems, this doesn't seem terribly farfetched, though the sun's "companion" star, if it exists, has never been observed. Perhaps, a few astronomers have suggested, this mysterious companion is a small but very dense star of a type known as a white dwarf, orbiting the sun at a very

*One extinction hypothesis is reflected
in this fanciful view of a dinosaur
watching an exploding meteor.*

great distance. It would be difficult, though not impossible, for astronomers to spot such a star, and it might pass through or near the Oort cloud on the required twenty-six-million-year cycle. A team of astronomers even suggested a name for this star: *Nemesis,* after the Greek goddess "who relentlessly persecutes the excessively rich, proud and powerful."[8]

Unfortunately, later calculations showed that Nemesis, if it exists, would have a highly unstable orbit around the sun and probably would have broken away long ago. It has also been suggested that Nemesis may have been "captured" by the sun only a half billion years or so ago, but this seems coincidental at best. Nonetheless, astronomers continue to search the sky looking for such a companion star.

Alternate theories attempting to explain the agitation of the Oort cloud suggest that it may be caused by a tenth planet orbiting beyond Pluto, or by the passage of the solar system through clouds of debris strewn through the disk of the galaxy.

The periodic extinctions theory is strikingly reminiscent of Cuvier's catastrophism, which we discussed in Chapter One. And many paleontologists feel that it should be discarded, as Cuvier's theories were, in light of a more uniformitarian hypothesis, an explanation of the extinction based more on the earthly cycles known to geologists.

At the moment, the best-grounded uniformitarian explanations of the extinctions have to do with changes in the earth's geography. These changes, in turn, are caused by the continental drift that we discussed in Chapter Two.

You'll recall that, at the beginning of the time of the dinosaurs, all of the earth's continents were grouped together in a single supercontinent, Pangaea. By the end of the Cretaceous, however, this supercontinent had broken up and begun drifting apart into the continents that we see on earth today.

Obviously, such a violent change in the nature of the continents would have affected the environment in which the dinosaurs lived. It would have disrupted the ability of the dinosaurs to migrate, for instance. As we suggested earlier, the dinosaurs may have migrated as birds did, and this may have been interrupted by the breakup of the continents.

Further, large inland seas would have drained back into the ocean. The loss of these seas, which would have retained heat during the winter and helped to make the changing seasons milder, would have made the climate much more erratic. Perhaps the dinosaurs were unable to adapt to these changes in the climate. The alterations of such sea environments might also explain the extinction of the reptiles and plants in the sea.

Similar changes in the geographic layout of the continents might explain other mass extinctions, though it would certainly not explain the twenty-six-million-year period detected by Raup and Sepkoski. However, this twenty-six-million-year period is highly controversial, and some paleontologists suspect that it is more of an accident of arithmetic than an actual cycle in the fossil record.

It is possible that we will *never* know the true reason for the dinosaur extinctions, or for many similar extinctions in the fossil record. Nonetheless, it is likely that new theories will arise to explain these mysterious episodes in the earth's distant past. Probably, the extinction was the result of a combination of factors, and so several of the theories that have been advanced to explain the disappearance of the dinosaurs may be true.

━━━━SEVEN━━━━
DINOSAUR
LEGACY

And so the dinosaurs vanished.

Inevitably, these fantastic reptiles have become linked in the public mind with evolutionary failure, as oversized lumbering beasts who were ultimately defeated at the hands of the smarter, more energetic, mammals. But this is hardly fair. The dinosaurs dominated the earth for more than 150 million years; the mammals have only been around for 65 million years and human beings for only 100,000 years or so. The dinosaurs were the most successful class of large animals yet fashioned by evolution. We don't yet know why they died out, but it is doubtful that they simply "failed," evolutionarily speaking.

We can thank our lucky stars that the dinosaurs no longer exist, however. Not only would a lumbering *Brachiosaurus* be an unwelcome guest at a backyard barbecue, but more advanced mammals such as human beings would almost certainly not have evolved if the dinosaurs' ecological niches had not been vacated. We owe our rise to the dinosaurs' demise.

Is it possible that not all dinosaurs became extinct? Could a few dinosaurs have survived, unbeknownst to human beings, into modern times? Periodically, there are reports of dinosaurlike creatures, such as the famous Loch Ness monster, that live in remote parts of the world. But there is no evidence that these creatures, if they exist at all, are descendants of survivors of the Mesozoic. The fossil record, in fact, indicates just the opposite. No dinosaur fossils have ever been found in strata higher than those of the Mesozoic, except in the few rare instances where the fossil record has been disrupted by subsequent geological activity. The dinosaurs were completely exterminated at the end of the Mesozoic by the mysterious forces of extinction.

Yet it has been suggested that dinosaurs may have survived in a form that each of us sees every day. *Birds* may well be the airborne descendants of the mighty reptiles of the Mesozoic.

The evidence for this possibility has been available for well over a century. In 1861, a startling fossil was discovered in a quarry in Bavaria. At first glance, it appeared to be the skeleton of a small dinosaur, but the rock in which the skeleton was buried held a clear impression of the "dinosaur's" flesh—and that flesh was covered with feathers!

Clearly, this skeleton (which was actually quite birdlike) was not that of a dinosaur but the

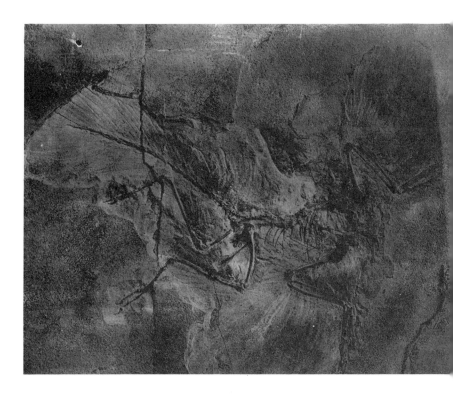

The fossil skeleton of Archaeopteryx,
*a primitive bird, shows a clear
resemblance to the early dinosaurs.*

skeleton of a bird, the earliest bird fossil ever discovered, dating from the late Triassic. Yet the resemblance to a dinosaur skeleton was overwhelming. This primitive bird, which was given the name *Archaeopteryx* ("ancient wing"), must have been a close relative of the early dinosaurs.

It was not immediately apparent how close this relationship was, however. It has never been doubted that birds descended from reptiles—a bird's feathers, for instance, seem to be a modification of the reptile's scales—but the identity of the specific ancestor of birds has never been determined.

At one point, it was suspected that birds descended from pterosaurs (which had already developed a mechanism for flying, after all). But *Archaeopteryx* made it seem more likely that birds had descended from a common ancestor with the dinosaurs, most likely from a species of thecodont.

Another *Archaeopteryx* was discovered in 1867; then, for nearly a century, no new skeletons of this primitive bird were found. Finally, in 1970, John Ostrom stumbled across another *Archaeopteryx* skeleton—in a museum in the Netherlands! The skeleton, which had actually been found in the 1850s, had been mislabeled as that of a pterosaur. Ostrom, however, recognized the mistake and had the skeleton shipped to his laboratory for closer examination. His studies showed Ostrom that this ancient bird bore a striking resemblance to the small coelurosaurian dinosaurs—much too great a resemblance to have resulted from common ancestry. *Archaeopteryx* was clearly a descendant of the dinosaurs, not of the thecodonts.

Although this theory is not accepted by all paleontologists, it is gaining wide currency. Robert Bakker, along with paleontologist Peter Galton, has gone so far as to suggest that modern birds, the descendants of *Archaeopteryx*, should be reclassified as a type of dinosaur. More specifically, Bakker and Galton have suggested that a new class of archosaur, the Dinosauria, should be created,

A restored Archaeopteryx *displays a richly feathered body.*

with subclasses called Ornithischia, Saurischia, and Aves (birds). Presently, the Ornithischia and Saurischia are considered separate orders of the subclass Archosauria—and birds are not considered to be archosaurs at all.

Of course, this is all a matter of names. Calling birds dinosaurs wouldn't *make* them dinosaurs, but it would certainly change the way that we perceive them. According to many paleontologists, the dinosaurs themselves were very birdlike, moving in a quick, darting manner, as birds do. When we see birds on the front lawn, then, we are seeing something that must look in many ways like the smaller dinosaurs did, except that we see feathers where an observer of the dinosaurs might have seen scales. And, in evolutionary terms, the distance from scales to feathers isn't all that great.

It's a pleasant thought. Perhaps the dinosaurs did not become extinct after all. It is not necessary to postulate Loch Ness monsters in order to bring the great Mesozoic reptiles back from the dead. Perhaps there is a dinosaur in your front yard right now or perched on a branch of the tree across the street. And just maybe you're going to have a dinosaur for dinner tonight. (It'll probably taste a lot like chicken.)

WHAT IF the Cretaceous extinction had never taken place, and the dinosaurs had not relinquished their ecological niches? Certainly, the dinosaurs would have evolved further, as the mammals did. Is it possible that, like the mammals, the dinosaurs would have evolved intelligence?

A few paleontologists have speculated on this possibility. In particular, a Canadian paleontologist named Dale Russell has speculated on the form that dinosaur intelligence might have taken. It is Russell's belief that intelligent dinosaurs might have descended from a late Cretaceous species of dinosaur called *Stenonychosaurus*, which had an unusually large brain case—a possible sign of high intelligence, by dinosaur standards, anyway.

Just as apelike creatures evolved into *Homo sapiens*, *Stenonychosaurus* may in time have evolved into an intelligent bipedal reptile that Russell calls a "dinosauroid." With the aid of a taxidermist named Ron Sequin, Russell has even constructed a fiberglass model of what he believed the dinosauroid might have looked like; this model is on view in the National Museum of Natural Sciences in Ottawa, Canada. In shape, it is strikingly humanoid, with arms, legs, and a neck very similar to those of human beings. But its skin is covered with scales, its hands have only three fingers, and its head is oddly shaped, with large oval-shaped eyes and virtually no jaw.

It is, of course, impossible to say whether dinosauroids would have evolved or if dinosaurs would indeed have developed into creatures with humanlike intelligence. Russell's dinosauroid is essentially science fiction, but it does help us to glimpse the infinite possibilities of evolution. Despite the now outmoded concept of the *Scala Naturae*, evolution does not necessarily lead to intelligence, just to better adaptations to a given environment. Dinosaurs were so well adapted to their environment that they survived for most of the era that we call the Mesozoic, and it may have been sudden changes in that environment that spelled the end of their time on earth.

Human fascination with the dinosaurs has persisted ever since the realization, in the mid-nineteenth century, that this planet was once dominated by a very special kind of large reptile. Perhaps we see in the dinosaurs a glimmer of our possible fate on this planet. We now dominate the earth much as the dinosaurs once did; but like that of the dinosaurs, our hold on this planet may be fragile. What hope do humans beings have of surviving as long as the dinosaurs did?

Our hope for such survival lies in the one thing that the dinosaurs did not have time to evolve—intelligence. One legacy of the dinosaurs is the knowledge that no species, no matter how successful, can dominate the earth forever. But unlike the dinosaurs, we are able to see the possibility of our own extinction lying on the road ahead of us, and we can do something about it. In reaching a better understanding of the dinosaurs, we are reaching a better understanding of our own possible fate.

NOTES AND
SOURCES USED

1. Quoted in John Noble Wilford, *The Riddle of the Dinosaur* (New York: Knopf, 1985), p. 173.
2. *Ibid.*, p. 167.
3. L.B. Halstead, *The Search for the Past* (New York: Double-day,1982), p. 134.
4. Robert Bakker, *The Dinosaur Heresies* (New York: Morrow, 1986), p. 389.
5. Halstead, *The Search for the Past*, p. 132.
6. John Ostrom, "Romancing the Dinosaurs," *The Sciences*, Vol. 27, No. 3, p. 63.
7. Quoted in Wilford, *The Riddle of the Dinosaur*, p. 215.
8. *Ibid.*, p. 258.

Asimov, Isaac. *Asimov's Biographical Encyclopedia of Science and Technology.* New York: Avon, 1972.
Bakker, Robert T. *The Dinosaur Heresies.* New York: Morrow, 1986.
Charig, Alan. *A New Look at the Dinosaurs.* New York: Facts on File, 1983.
Colbert, Edwin H. *Dinosaurs: An Illustrated History.* Maplewood, N.J.: Hammond, 1983.
———.*The Great Dinosaur Hunters and Their Discoveries* [formerly *Men and Dinosaurs*]. New York: Dover, 1984.

Desmond, Adrian J. *The Hot-Blooded Dinosaurs*. New York: Dial Press, 1976.

Eiseley, Loren. *Darwin's Century*. New York: Doubleday, 1958.

Halstead, L.B. *The Search for the Past*. New York: Doubleday, 1982.

Lewin, Roger. *Thread of Life: The Smithsonian Looks at Evolution*. Washington, D.C.: Smithsonian Books, 1982.

Morell, Virginia, "Announcing the Birth of a Heresy." *Discover* (March 1987), Vol. 8, No. 3, p. 26.

Ostrom, John, "Romancing the Dinosaurs." *The Sciences* (May/June 1987), Vol. 27, No. 3, p. 56.

Reader, John. *The Rise of Life: The First 3.5 Billion Years*. New York: Knopf, 1986.

Rudwick, Martin J.S. *The Meaning of Fossils: Episodes in the History of Paleontology*. Chicago: University of Chicago Press, 1985.

Wilford, John Noble. *The Riddle of the Dinosaur*. New York: Knopf, 1985.

RECOMMENDED
READING

From the 1850s, when Richard Owen gave the "terrible lizards" their name, down to the present day, the dinosaurs
have captured the public imagination in a way that no other
extinct class of animals ever has, and the literature on dinosaurs has grown accordingly. The books written about these
ancient reptiles certainly number in the thousands, ranging
from coloring books for preschoolers to technical expositions
unreadable by anyone but the experienced paleontologist.
The list of recommended books that follows is necessarily
incomplete, representing only the most interesting or significant volumes that the author of the present work encoun-
tered in his research. However, if you are interested in
current theories of warm-blooded dinosaurs, two of the
books—those by Desmond and Bakker—are indispensable.
Bakker, in particular, describes these theories and their sup-
porting arguments in considerable detail. Bear in mind while
reading these two books, however, that they are heavily biased in favor of these ideas and make it sound as though the
theories of dinosaur warm-bloodedness, which are extremely controversial among paleontologists, are more firmly
grounded in fossil evidence than they actually are. Readers
in search of a more basic introduction to dinosaurs than is
provided by Bakker and Desmond will want to read the
books by Colbert, Charig, and Wilford.

The Hot-Blooded Dinosaurs by Adrian Desmond (New York: Dial Press, 1976).

This is the book that introduced the new theories of dinosaur warm-bloodedness to the general public. Although it is not recommended as an introduction for the uninitiated reader, Desmond provides a vivid if somewhat slanted look at how the dinosaurs and their various species evolved. Note that the original American edition [1976] is printed in dark red-black ink, perhaps to keep the reader in a hot-blooded frame of mind.

The Dinosaur Heresies by Robert T. Bakker, Ph.D. (New York: Morrow, 1986).

A catalog of revisionist dinosaur theories, written by their most outspoken proponent. Most paleontologists, including Bakker's own teacher and mentor, John Ostrom, regard Bakker's views on dinosaur physiology as much too extreme, but there is little question that he is the liveliest contemporary writer on the subject. The second chapter, where Bakker describes the fossil record as it appears to a dinosaur hunter in the field, should be required reading for the budding paleontologist. Some of the material in succeeding chapters may seem a bit overly detailed to the casual reader, but Bakker's prose style and descriptions of complex phenomena are always lucid and interesting.

A New Look at the Dinosaurs by Alan Charig (New York: Facts on File, 1983).

A good overall look at dinosaurs and paleontology by a British expert. Appropriate for a reader not already familiar with the subject.

Dinosaurs: An Illustrated History by Edwin H. Colbert (Maplewood, N.J.: Hammond, 1983).

Colbert is not only the dean of twentieth-century dinosaur hunters but also one of the most prolific writers of popular books on the subject. Any book by Colbert is recommended; this is the most recent. Although not as detailed as some of Colbert's earlier books, it is a good introduction to the subject of dinosaurs in general, with (as the title implies) a large number of illustrations.

The Great Dinosaur Hunters and Their Discoveries by Edwin H. Colbert (New York: Dover, 1984).

A classic history of dinosaur paleontology, with vivid biographical sketches of Gideon Mantell, Edward Drinker Cope, Othniel Charles Marsh, Charles Sternberg, Roy Chapman Andrews, and other great dinosaur hunters. In its original edition, entitled *Men and Dinosaurs* [1968], this book was used as source material by many of the other authors in this listing.

The Search for the Past by L.B. Halstead (New York: Doubleday, 1982).

A general introduction to fossils and paleontology by a British paleontologist and geologist. The illustrations are excellent, and the description of how the fossil record is formed is especially good.

Digging Dinosaurs by John R. Horner and James Gorman (New York: Workman, 1988).

Horner, one of the top modern dinosaur hunters, relates his experiences.

The Riddle of the Dinosaur by John Noble Wilford (New York: Knopf, 1985).

An extremely readable introduction to dinosaur paleontology by a science correspondent for the *New York Times*. Wilford concentrates more on the paleontologists than on the dinosaurs themselves, but he offers a vivid picture of how current ideas about dinosaurs developed and puts the debate about warm-blooded dinosaurs into perspective. He devotes an unusual amount of space to the debate over the Cretaceous extinction, especially concerning the asteroid- and comet-impact theories.

INDEX